LIFE SUPPORT
A Survival Guide for the Modern Soul

Derek Draper

HAY HOUSE

Australia • Canada • Hong Kong • India
South Africa • United Kingdom • United States

First published and distributed in the United Kingdom by:
Hay House UK Ltd, 292B Kensal Rd, London W10 5BE. Tel.: (44) 20 8962 1230;
Fax: (44) 20 8962 1239. www.hayhouse.co.uk

Published and distributed in the United States of America by:
Hay House, Inc., PO Box 5100, Carlsbad, CA 92018-5100. Tel.: (1) 760 431 7695 or (800)
654 5126; Fax: (1) 760 431 6948 or (800) 650 5115. www.hayhouse.com

Published and distributed in Australia by:
Hay House Australia Ltd, 18/36 Ralph St, Alexandria NSW 2015. Tel.: (61) 2 9669 4299;
Fax: (61) 2 9669 4144. www.hayhouse.com.au

Published and distributed in the Republic of South Africa by:
Hay House SA (Pty), Ltd, PO Box 990, Witkoppen 2068. Tel./Fax: (27) 11 467 8904.
www.hayhouse.co.za

Published and distributed in India by:
Hay House Publishers India, Muskaan Complex, Plot No.3, B-2, Vasant Kunj, New Delhi –
110 070. Tel.: (91) 11 4176 1620; Fax: (91) 11 4176 1630. www.hayhouse.co.in

Distributed in Canada by:
Raincoast, 9050 Shaughnessy St, Vancouver, BC V6P 6E5. Tel.: (1) 604 323 7100;
Fax: (1) 604 323 2600

A catalogue record for this book is available from the British Library.

ISBN 978-1-84850-044-0

Printed in the UK by CPI William Clowes Beccles, NR34 7TL

Contents

Part I – Understanding You

Understanding Your Inner World   3

Don't underestimate the power of the inner world – it colours how we see ourselves and our perception of the world around us.

Finding Direction   7

Do you feel your life has no meaning? If so, what can you do about it? Look for a feeling of 'rightness' and you'll know you're on the right path.

Telling the Truth   11

How can you tell if you're lying to yourself? If you've been clinging to a false reality, it's time to understand why.

Remembering Right   15

Everyone has memories of key events in their past, yet sometimes we invent traumas as well as hide them. What can we learn from what we remember?

Part 3 – Understanding Your World

Part 4 – Understanding Therapy

Acknowledgements

There are many people to thank, and most of them – my patients – must go unnamed. From my first, the shy 17-year-old in California who wanted nothing more than someone to show some interest in him, to the ones I see each week now. The hope is, of course, that they learn something from me, but again and again it is I who am wiser after the work we do together. This book is as much their gift as mine.

My own therapists over the last decade – Lois, Michael, Dr Keller, Dr Taylor and Dr Galatarioutou – have helped me in very different but profound ways. My supervisors at different times – Jessica, Mike, Peter, Laurie, Terry, David, Deborah, Brett and especially Susie – have been crucial to my growth as a therapist; similarly, any wisdom in this book is as much – if not more – theirs than mine. The same applies to those colleagues who have become close friends: Caroline and Cecilia.

I also owe thanks to Hachette and *Psychologies* magazine, who gave me the opportunity to first write in such depth about psychotherapy. Maureen Rice and Clare Longrigg have been the best editors a writer could wish for.

Outside the professional world, my own parents, Ken and Chrina, gave – and give – me so much. But for her seemingly limitless love and support I reserve, as always, my deepest thanks for Kate, my true beloved. I dedicate this book to her – and our little girl Darcey.

Introduction

Every day, psychotherapy helps thousands of people: they feel happier, achieve more success and enjoy better relationships. But not everyone can – or wants to – be in therapy. The good news is that dozens of tips and tools from the therapy room are available for you to use right now. In this book I explore over 40 issues that impact on almost everyone's lives and, using examples drawn from everyday life, seek a better understanding of why things happen, offering clear insights and advice that will help you think about life's challenges in new, more positive ways. The stories in this book will hopefully inspire you to change the way you think, feel and behave and show you how to be a better wife, husband, parent and friend. Above all, though, they will help you become a better *you* – because the more we understand why we do what we do, the more we can change ourselves for the better and enjoy the fuller, happier lives we deserve.

(Any case examples used are fictionalized and therefore do not refer to any specific individual case. These are always strictly confidential.)

PART I

UNDERSTANDING YOU

Understanding Your Inner World

Don't underestimate the power of the inner world – it colours how we see ourselves and our perception of the world around us.

In my consulting room I see a succession of women who, from the outside, seem to have it all: youth, looks, brains, a great job, money in the bank and a thrilling social life. But these same women are often wrecked with insecurity. To them, looking from the inside, they are dumb, boring and ugly.

It is a phenomenon that doesn't just appear in therapy. We all know people who suffer in this way, and we know that no matter how much we bolster their self-confidence, the effects don't last.

What could possibly cause this tragic dissonance between what people appear to be to the outside world, and what they believe and feel on the inside?

One of the great discoveries of psychoanalysis provides an answer. For we do not live in one world, but two: the outer world consists of other people, objects and nature, while the inner world is made up of our feelings, beliefs and dreams. Sometimes we call the first world 'reality'. But we couldn't be more wrong. Both worlds are equally real. Moreover, when it comes to determining how we feel about ourselves, it is the second world that provides the tone and mood music by which we live our lives, not the first.

This is illustrated by one of the most famous psychological tests – the Rorschach, or inkblot test. I had to practise giving the test to my fellow students when I was studying for my MA in psychology in America. Examinees are shown a series of symmetrical patterns, formed, literally, by random inkblots. But the image, by definition, isn't 'anything', so what we see on the card in front of us has to come from inside our own minds – what psychologists call 'projection'. Our responses thus reveal how we colour the world.

I gave the test first to a woman we'll call Juliet. She looked upon the weirdly-shaped stain and began to smile. 'Oh wow!' she exclaimed. 'It's two real funny clowns. They are dancing around, waving flowers in the air and all around them are beautiful butterflies dancing around in the sun.'

The next day I showed the exact same card to Sally. Her brow darkened. At first she wouldn't speak. Eventually she whispered, 'There are two terrible witches and they are shooting machine guns at each other. Blood and body parts are splattering the air around them.'

From hanging out with these women at our Institute, I could see this dramatic difference played out. Both women were highly intelligent, very attractive and interesting company. But Juliet had a sunny disposition, always seeing the

good in situations, possibly to extremes. Sally spent much of her time being grumpy, feeling threatened and acting self-destructively.

One came from a secure, loving family and was in constant contact with her parents, who were still together. The other's father had left her mother when she was 12, after years of drinking and abuse, and her mother would, even to that day, compete with her to be the prettiest and most popular with men. No prizes for guessing which of my fellow students came from which home.

That is the reason why the mood music from our internal worlds proves so insistent. It is a track that is laid down in our childhoods, when we are most sensitive to what others think of us. It is from our parents and sometimes other close relatives that we hear the chorus that accompanies our developing lives: 'She's a moody one;' 'He'll never amount to anything;' 'She twists everyone around her little finger.' Sometimes, of course, there's some truth to these labels, but often they originate not in external reality – what the child is actually doing – but are projections from the internal world of the parent. Then, tragically, the label can become a self-fulfilling prophecy: the indistinct figure 'becomes' the clown or the evil witch.

Good therapy is about uncovering these often unconscious, ingrained assumptions, and replacing them with a more realistic appraisal. But it can be a long and painful task – and opens one up to powerful feelings of anger, guilt and, this time, genuine self-criticism.

Anger, because facing up to the damage that has been done to you – by those you depended on most – can tap into reservoirs of rage repressed for decades.

Guilt, because most parents combine their damaging projections with a degree of love and support that leaves the grown-up child confused – who am I to complain and criticize?

And genuine self-criticism, because a more realistic appraisal of oneself usually involves facing up to genuine shortcomings that were once hidden under blanket self-immolation, and that require real work to put right.

A friend of mine puts himself down constantly, always suggesting that he has failed as a friend. In fact he is usually loyal and decent, but occasionally does let me down. My objections to this are lost in his blanket wail of self-criticism.

Despite these difficulties, we do need to deal with that childhood legacy, for only if we heal our damaged internal worlds will we be able to enjoy our achievements in the external one. Otherwise, our success will only ever be skin deep.

Suggested Resource

What's Wrong With You – Seven Logical Steps to Understanding Emotional Illusions by Benjamin Fry (Maraki Books) – or visit www.benjaminfry.co.uk

Finding Direction

Do you feel your life has no meaning? If so, what can you do about it? Look for a feeling of 'rightness' and you'll know you're on the best path.

Discussions on finding direction in life usually leapfrog over a key initial question that any navigator would tell you has to be considered before anything else: am I really lost? Because sometimes it feels as if we have lost our way, but just around the corner is the place we've always wanted to be.

We have to be aware that life will not always feel as if it is on a smooth, upward, simple trajectory. All of us will feel adrift at some point in our lives. Indeed, if we don't it probably means that we are too driven. So it's OK to have fallow periods, where we rest and recharge. But these times should alternate with phases of being more active, and the general route should be leading us somewhere. In other words, we can plateau out occasionally, but we should still have the summit in our sights.

So how do we know if we've hit a plateau, or are struggling up the wrong mountain altogether?

Just as with actual physical travel, our psychic journey can be guided by the points of the compass, only the letters stand for different things. I think there are four elements, matching the four points N, E, S and W, which are always present if we have found our purpose. If they are not, then we need to do some pretty fundamental self-examination. Without them, we are in danger of just existing rather than truly living.

N stands for *natural*. If we have found our groove, it feels good. What psychologists call flow, or athletes call the zone. If what we are doing doesn't feel right, at least most of the time, then it isn't.

E represents the related idea of *energy*. Having purpose doesn't remove struggles and setbacks, but when we are on the right path we somehow manage to survive these. Reserves of enthusiasm and faith follow in the wake of knowing where we are going and why. We have a great capacity to 'bounce back'.

S conjures up the concept of *soul*. Our true path lies in something which invigorates not just our bank balance or our social life but something deeper, more spiritual. We feel, deep within us, that we are at peace.

W relates to the notion of *work*. If we have found our vocation – professionally, socially or relationally – we will find that the work involved comes easy. We might get exhausted but we will also feel, a lot of the time, exhilarated.

For me, my early involvement in politics gave my life meaning. But eventually these elements fell away. First I felt I'd lost my soul, then my work didn't come naturally any

more; it began to feel alien. Then I ceased to be able to work at all and lost my energy, eventually breaking down and becoming depressed.

As I recovered, I tried different things. A stint in Talk Radio came naturally, but I never felt energized by it. Setting up an advertising agency was motivating in a sense, but none of it was organic, and the activity itself felt soulless. I feel lucky to have rediscovered all four elements in my work as a therapist, but it wasn't a straightforward journey.

I think there are three vital steps to finding a new direction if you feel you may have lost yours. The first is to make sure it's really happened. Audit the above four elements. Which are missing from your life? Second, accept that you are going through a difficult patch, and if necessary seek help from a therapist or good life-coach. At the very least be ready to put in the contemplation and self-analysis required to change. Third, have the strength to leap a little into the unknown. Try some new things, abandon past prejudices. Allow yourself what economists call a period of creative destruction. Phoenixes, as we know, emerge from ashes. We have to be brave enough to admit something has burned up in us, and accept the loss, before we can fly again.

Suggested Resource

Re-inventing Your Life: How to Break Free from Negative Life Patterns by Jeffrey E. Young and Janet S. Klosko (Penguin)

Telling the Truth

How can you tell if you're lying to yourself? If you've been clinging to a false reality, it's time to understand why.

Whole lives can be built on lies. We see the most dramatic manifestations of this in those high-profile cases of bigamists, or fantasists who confer fictitious titles or riches upon themselves. But more subtle variations are often seen in therapists' consulting rooms, and when they occur, they present a great challenge.

There are essentially two types of lying. The first is the 'knowing' lie – the conscious, deliberate falsehood. It can be told with the best of intentions – the white lie – or the worst. In our very worst moments, when we knowingly lie to steal an advantage, we may even secretly glory in our mendacity. More usually, though, we try to bury the memory of the deed, or distract ourselves from the guilt, because it's too uncomfortable to live with the lie.

The second type of dishonesty, however, occurs when we cannot live *without* our lie. This is the 'unknown' lie.

What happens here is that we have to believe in something, even against all the evidence, because it is too precious to us to forgo. The clichéd example – and it's a cliché because it so often happens – is the patient who enters therapy and reports a blissful childhood and perfect, loving parents. They are deeply rooted to the belief; for them, it is almost literally an article of faith. Only as the work unfolds does another, very different, story of their family emerge, which is at best mixed and at worst terribly traumatic.

If a therapist confronts the lie head-on it can be disastrous, and lead to a collapse of the therapy. This is because the lie has often become necessary over the course of many years, acting as a defence against some knowledge that would be too unbearable if confronted directly. The lie has become a vital, self-preserving belief.

At its best, therapy should gently but firmly begin to bring this new story of what really happened in their childhood into contact with the conflicting assertion of blissful happiness. For a while the two versions may have to sit side by side, until there is a gradual reconciliation, at which point the patient can finally acknowledge – in the safety of the therapeutic relationship – that things were not as they have forced themselves to believe. A crucial part of the process, though, is for the patient to feel compassionate towards the part of them that had to lie, and to understand how that lie was vital; how it protected them from a pain or anger which would have been literally unbearable.

What, then, is the best clue that a patient's original version of events is not the whole story? There is a useful test which can help determine the truth of what someone 'believes' – and it can be helpful for all of us, not just those in the therapist's chair. It involves something I call 'asynchronic affect'. A patient who claims to recall a blissful early life is probably near to the truth if he or she accompanies the assertion with bright eyes, a grin, and lots of supporting anecdotes and detail. Often, however, what happens is that they talk about their 'loving parents' with empty eyes and wan, wistful sighs, and cannot offer a single illustration to back it up. They may speak the lie, but their face gives away the truth.

It is a test that we can all apply to ourselves. When we tell ourselves something, do we find ourselves feeling the appropriate emotions? Or, if we look and listen closely, do we realize we are feeling something quite different – or even not very much at all? If you are not sure whether some of your long-held assumptions and beliefs are really true, or are in fact 'unknown' lies, try and take the affect test yourself. Think or say aloud your 'truth', and pay close attention to how it makes you feel. Examine your own body language; what is your stomach telling you? Are your hands clenched or calm? Do you feel light or heavy? Is your mouth twitching into a smile, or set in a line? As Oprah Winfrey puts it, 'Love ain't supposed to feel bad.'

If there is a dissonance between the 'truth' and what your body is telling you, then it's time to reflect on whether you might, in this particular instance, be living a lie. If you are, then it is time to try and understand why.

Suggested Resource

Vital Lies, Simple Truths: Psychology of Self-deception by Daniel Goleman (Bloomsbury)

Remembering Right

Everyone has memories of key events in their past, yet sometimes we invent traumas as well as hide them. What can we learn from what we remember?

When you start therapy, the first thing a good therapist will do is take your 'personal history' – details of your family, childhood and key events that have shaped who you are today.

Often, midway through therapy I will look back on these initial notes and it is astonishing how often they fail to tell the whole story, and in some cases are actually misleading. Siblings have been omitted, major childhood illnesses erased, parental neglect or abuse wished away. One time, a marriage didn't merit a mention.

There can be different reasons for this. Sometimes it's just because the memory is embarrassing and the client isn't ready to share it in that often anxiety-provoking initial meeting. But often the memory has effectively been laid aside. It is no longer part of the person's personal narrative.

In the film *Total Recall*, the Arnold Schwarzenegger character is interrogated about why he wants his memory back. 'To be myself again,' he replies. But it doesn't work so simply. We assume our memories make us who we are, but actually, a lot of the time who we are makes our memories.

Psychological researchers have long discredited our commonly held assumptions about memory. Tests show that if you are given a convincing story of something that happened in your past and are asked to think about it over the course of a few weeks, you will later swear you can remember the events, even when told it is a false memory.

Other studies reveal that people mis-remember key events when these are checked against historical data. Quite a few of us don't remember where we were when we heard about the World Trade Centre on 11 September 2001; we just think we do.

Other researchers have shown that manipulative words used to question people about events can lead to people embroidering their memories. Such experiments have revealed people swearing they saw a 'Stop' sign when it was actually a 'Give Way', or recalling that a clean-shaven man had a moustache and that a bald man had curly hair.

Jean Piaget, a renowned Swiss child psychologist, tells a revealing story in his memoirs:

> *I can still see, most clearly, the following scene, which*
> *I believed until I was about fifteen. I was sitting in my*
> *pram, which my nurse was pushing in the Champs*

*Elysées, when a man tried to kidnap me. I was held
in by the strap fastened around me while my nurse
bravely tried to stand between me and the thief. She
received various scratches, and I can still see vaguely
those on her face. Then a crowd gathered, a police-
man with a short cloak and a white baton came
up, and the man took to his heels. I can still see the
whole scene, and can even place it near the tube
station.*

This is the kind of traumatic memory that might be part
of someone's personal history, or emerge in therapy. But
Piaget goes on:

*When I was about fifteen, my parents received a
letter from my former nurse saying that she had
been converted to the Salvation Army. She wanted
to confess her past faults, and in particular to return
the watch she had been given on this occasion. She
had made up the whole story, faking the scratches. I,
therefore, must have heard, as a child, the account of
this story, which my parents believed, and projected it
into my memory.*

So, in a courtroom and in the consulting room, we have
to be wary of our memories. They may not be as accurate
a historical record as we'd like to think. However, they are
still extremely useful. For while they may not reveal what

actually happened, they tell us a great deal about what we *wanted* to happen, or felt *had* to have happened. They are the pieced-together explanations of who we are and why.

That is why, in the course of therapy, one is always wise to be wary of specific memories, and should always be asking the question, 'What purpose does this memory serve?'

Most of the time, the memories we have of our childhood and parents are a little slanted. We've told ourselves the tale so often that it becomes one-dimensional, a little cartoonish. Usually, therapy involves an analysis of these memories that yields another side to the story. For as much as emotional development may require us to recover certain memories, it often also requires us to let go of some too.

Suggested Resource

Essentials of Human Memory by Alan D. Baddeley (Psychology Press)

Letting Go

Ever found yourself unable to let go of something close to you – a doomed love, a job you hate, a house that's too big? Let's look at why sometimes we can't move on.

A few years ago a friend of mine was invited to lunch with Gordon Brown and his aides at No 11 Downing Street. They discussed Brown's then neighbour, Tony Blair, and when he might finally quit. Someone – my friend won't confirm it was Brown himself – claimed that Tony Blair would cling to office because he had a 'psychological hang-up about leaving'.

Not being able to let go of something when circumstances mean you have to is a problem that recurs endlessly in the therapist's consulting room. The partner who perseveres – for years – in a relationship in which she feels belittled and stifled; the man who stays in a job that saps his energy and mocks his integrity; the woman who remains preoccupied by the slights handed down by her father decades ago. The list is endless.

My type of therapy holds that we are unique, complicated creatures, and that each of these people hangs on to a thought, feeling or situation for complex reasons. But over time I have identified a common dynamic that almost always plays a part in this condition.

When we think consciously that we are stuck in a certain way of being – what Freud called the repetition compulsion or the 'fate' neurosis – we are often unconsciously seeking to put right something that has gone wrong.

This can be healthy. Mourning is a process in which we repeatedly call up memories of our dead loved one, each provoking an outpouring of grief until gradually the impact of a come-upon snapshot or favourite song being played on the radio diminishes.

When I worked with children in California, they would often relive painful experiences through their play. One little girl used the plastic figure of a man to act out him leaving whatever game was going on. She was trying to come to terms, week in and week out, with her father's abandonment of her and her mother.

This sort of repetition should allow healing to take place, and an eventual moving on. But Freud noticed that sometimes this didn't happen, and the person became fixated, locked into their fate and unable to escape it.

I think this happens when people, often without realizing it, blame themselves in some way for what has happened. They are unconsciously punishing themselves by not moving on, and also trying, desperately and with almost no chance of success, to make things different. Deep down,

they are dreaming that one day their partner, job or parents will finally stop disappointing them, and transform into what they've always needed and wanted.

In the meantime – and this is what gives such paralysis its vicious undertow – they stay impaled, punishing themselves for their part in creating such a mess.

If you find yourself stuck in a situation and unable to move on, you may simply be frightened of change. But there is probably something deeper going on. Ask yourself if, deep down, you have really given up, or are you secretly hoping for a miracle to put things right; and then ask whether, in the meantime, you might be punishing yourself for your part in your downfall.

Staying in a situation, however painful, can be a great distraction from the loss, guilt and self-blame that are bound to accompany actually moving on – as opposed to just dreaming about it.

Tony Blair is, in a way, lucky. He was eventually forced to move on. Many of us, though, are perfectly capable of remaining stuck for ever, wound up in a terrible cocktail of wishful thinking and masochism, because we are so desperate to avoid the downside of progress – pain over what we have wasted. Of course, we also then risk missing out on the upside: the possibility of something exciting and new.

Suggested Resource

The Language of Letting Go Journal by Melody Beattie (Hazelden)

Getting Angry

If you don't get in touch with your feelings of anger and aggression, they might just surface in unexpected ways.

I get paid by women to make them hate me. And get angry with me, and envious of me. They don't always know that it's happening, but I believe it is an intrinsic part of what they are 'buying' when they enter my consulting room – because therapy without any bad thoughts and feelings isn't really therapy at all. Therapy without anger or hate is like the Grand National without Beecher's Brook. And yet, many women in therapy have enormous difficulty dealing with what Freudians call our 'aggressive drive'.

If I remember some detail of a patient's life incorrectly, or forget something important, or am insensitive (and those things can happen at some time or another), I *want* my patient to get cross with me. A minority – usually men – go through their whole lives ranting and raving, so they are more than happy to pick fault with me in a session, even when I feel blameless. But a much larger number, and it's particularly true of women, have the opposite problem. Everything in their eyes is their own fault. Excuses must always be made for other people's bad behaviour. There is literally nothing they won't do to avoid a confrontation.

All too often, these women have blurred the distinction between thought and deed. The simple act of having a 'bad' thought seems as awful to them as carrying it out — so they cannot allow themselves to have angry feelings, and must censor even their own most private thoughts. The goal of psychotherapy isn't to turn these women into proto-Russell Crowes, hurling telephones around. Therapy helps them get in touch with angry feelings, not in order for them to act upon them, but to feel OK about simply having them.

So what if you sometimes want to kill your sister because she's got a baby and you haven't? So what if (sharp intake of breath) it once flashed across your mind that you'd like to throttle the cute little bundle itself? That doesn't make you evil. It just makes you normal. Long before the advent of psychotherapy, women's darker feelings were finding subtle expression through other means. Think of the generations of mothers who have whispered 'Rock-a-bye-baby' to their beloved offspring: 'When the bough breaks, the cradle will fall, and down will come baby, cradle and all.'

Feminism told us, rightly, that society acts to take away women's power. I am sure that plays a part in contributing to women's discomfort with their own aggression. Daughters often inherit unease and guilt about anger from their own mothers. The unspoken message is not just that

women shouldn't think bad thoughts, but – and this is what gives the idea its potency – that such bad thoughts 'spoil' their good thoughts. Women grow up believing they cannot be viciously envious of others and at the same time want to take loving care of them, so one of the two feelings must be banished. 'Good girls don't get mad,' goes the saying – just as inaccurate as 'Big boys don't cry.'

The trouble is, feelings can't be banished. It simply isn't possible. All you can ever do is bury them – but what happens to all that disavowed female anger? It assumes a disguise and resurfaces, most commonly as passive aggression. All of those subtle, often silent devices we use to get back at people without having to admit to our feelings – often without even recognizing what we're doing – are symptoms of passive aggression. Hence those most bitter of rows, when one partner feels genuinely attacked and slighted, while the other feels genuinely innocent.

I think it also surfaces in behaviours that seem superficially harmless but are not, such as gossiping. The bitchiness of the high-school girls I used to treat in California was just as vicious as the overt bullying among the boys. Being cast out by the in-crowd can be just as painful as a good kicking, if not more so.

As well as disguising itself, buried aggression can also redirect itself – almost invariably turning inward. Self-destructive behaviour including drinking, drug use and overspending are classic examples – but it can also be expressed through a pattern of destructive relationships. A host of other symptoms, such as depression, anxiety and eating disorders, are often fed by 'anger turned inwards'. The sufferer isn't aware of this, and so can't see that the way to break free is to locate their aggression, own it, become comfortable with it and eventually learn that it isn't going to destroy anybody, if only it is acknowledged.

This need for an internal emotional balance, which accepts all of our impulses, good and bad, is reflected in the Eastern notion of *yin* and *yang*. The prize goes beyond saving yourself from the harm that all that unowned aggression can do to your life. It also does something to our capacity to own the good things too. In order to experience any emotion, I believe we need to be comfortable feeling *all* of them. If you can't acknowledge what Jung labelled your 'shadow' – your hate, anger and envy – then you end up not being able to fully experience love, joy or kindness.

Sigmund Freud, despite his cold reputation, once wrote to a friend that cure, in therapy, comes through love. I think that is true. But psychic health and emotional wellbeing also come through hate, and from the realization that we can love and hate the same person, and that such hate need not destroy that love, but can actually make it stronger.

Suggested Resource

Overcoming Anger and Irritability by William Davies (Robinson Publishing)

Letting It All Out

Anger can be positive and empowering, so why do we find it so hard to express?

It is a cliché, but for good reason: every therapist is hoping that their patient will end up having a good cry. Usually they do. Sadness, although it can be buried deep within us, is almost always reachable with good therapy. Feeling safe enough to cry and work through the pain is a sign that therapy is working.

Other emotions, too, invariably make an appearance during most treatments: worry, fear, jealousy and, fingers crossed, joy and hope too. But there is another emotion that can prove particularly elusive: anger. That tells us something, I think, about our society well beyond the consulting room.

It seems to me that many of us, and society as a whole in a way, split our approach to anger into two extremes. We either bury it, allowing ourselves to be pushed around, or we explode with pent-up rage at the slightest provocation.

Take a patient of mine who suffered terribly during her childhood. There had never been any overt physical or sexual abuse, but her upper-middle-class parents had simply hardly ever been there: her dad was always at the office and her mum out with friends, or, when she was at home, inebriated.

This patient knew she'd missed out, and was able to be very sad at the loneliness she felt, and still feels, as a result of her parents' emotional neglect. But she can't get angry with them. I have tried deep questioning, visualizations and role play, but anger comes there none. Yet she is terribly bitter about life, and has a generally hostile attitude.

She also rages at shop assistants, parking wardens and, with serious consequences, assistants at work, which I strongly suspect is fuelled by her underlying anger with her parents. Despite her not being able to make any connection between her deep-rooted anger and her behaviour, we have made some progress with her rage attacks, using a simple, four-word tool that I use often with patients.

This involves remembering just four words. The words represent four actions which, if you religiously go through them when you feel an anger attack coming on, will invariably calm you down.

The words are:
STOP
BREATHE
REFLECT
CHOOSE.

The first two are pretty self-explanatory. REFLECT means just have a think about what you are about to do and why, and how you'll feel afterwards. CHOOSE represents the option you have at this point: do you really want to do this? Do you really want to carry on like this?

Great though it is to see this patient of mine erupt less often, I fear we are not getting to the root of her problems, and need to keep digging. We have to find a way for her to express her anger healthily without her feeling it will be overwhelming. I suspect that she feels that if she lets it out she will destroy herself and the people she's angry with, whom she also, of course, deep down still needs to love. That is why I need to keep reinforcing the simple message: it's OK to be angry with people. It doesn't destroy them and it won't destroy you.

This isn't about getting angry with people to their face – though you might choose to do that, in a careful and con-trolled way – but about being angry in private, or in therapy. *Feeling* the emotion is the important thing, not necessarily *acting* on it, and of course, as with all things, we do need to be respectful of others and seek a healthy balance.

We have demonized anger in our society. I sometimes wonder if the resistance I see in the consulting room, and its negative effects, are mirrored more widely. Maybe if we let off steam now and again there'd be less road rage, casual and domestic violence, self-harm, and even – and I am being serious – fewer high-school shootings. Maybe even, one day, fewer wars.

But the change has to start within each of us. We need to get comfortable with the odd bit of stomping, shouting and swearing – and we need to get used to being on the receiving end of that, too.

'Better out than in' is another therapist's cliché, and it's never truer than when said of anger. It is the loudest and most dramatic of emotions. Just think of the power of someone when they are showing righteous anger. Then think how much damage we must do to ourselves if we repress all that and turn it inwards. No wonder we eventually explode.

Suggested Resource

Overcoming Anger: When Anger Helps and When It Hurts by Windy Dryden (Sheldon Press)

Acting Your Age

It's part of being a teenager to mope and have tantrums as we search to find our true selves. Let's explore why our adolescent mental behaviour can stretch into adulthood.

Simple maths tells you it shouldn't last more than seven years. But as primary school kids mimic children twice their age, and the middle-aged hijack the style, music and even the language of adolescence, the teenage years seem set to colonize an ever-increasing slice of our lives.

From a psychological viewpoint, though, the arrested adolescence that matters doesn't concern the urge to don teenage trappings, but the more profound phenomenon of an inability to move beyond the adolescent developmental stage.

The famous psychoanalyst Erik Ericson identified seven ages of man, and believed that each stage involved the mastery of a particular question. Adolescence, he thought, revolved around defining oneself: developing a stable identity and self-image.

Not successfully navigating this period doesn't necessarily leave you wearing cargo pants and listening to hip hop on your iPod, but it does leave you asking that question posed in thousands of therapists' consulting rooms across the world: who am I?

I think that a successful navigation of the trials and temptations of adolescence – and thus the resolving of Erikson's developmental task – is actually determined long before it even begins.

For the lack of a real sense of self – What kind of person am I? What do I really enjoy? Where am I really going? And why? – is often caused by difficulties experienced much earlier in childhood than the teenage years. Most often it is the result of one of two opposite but related parental failings (getting the balance right between the two is the art of successful child-rearing).

On the one hand, some parents are devastatingly absent – physically or emotionally – and therefore cannot act as a sounding board for their child's emotional and intellectual strivings. An unrecognized, unmirrored child is a child who never develops the moorings necessary to safely explore and determine who they are.

At the other extreme there are parents who are *too* involved – impinging on a child's space to try out different attitudes and approaches. These parents are often living out their own frustrated yearnings through their kids. To see such a dynamic in cringe-making close-up, watch Channel Five's *Showbiz Moms and Dads*.

The solid psychological foundation a child needs is laid in the years – thank goodness – before the chemical and hormonal chaos of puberty. That is why some teenagers go off the rails completely and others merely look like they might for a while.

The extent to which a child has a positive, loving core sense of themselves – and the self-esteem that goes with it – explains the difference between a child who looks like a punk for a few years and one that becomes completely lost in a punk subculture of nihilism and alienation.

Where this ties up with the problems of many adults who seek therapy, or feel they are living empty lives, is that although they may not get completely 'lost' in adolescence they enter adulthood with a key part of themselves missing: the deep sense 'in their bones', as another renowned psychoanalyst, Donald Winnicott, put it, of who they are.

Hence, I think, the allure of the signifiers of teenagedom. Through these it is possible for people to enter a prolonged 'adultescence' where they fail to acknowledge how lost they are, and stay absorbed in a world of adolescent preoccupations and dramas. Constantly seeking an identity provides a great distraction from owning up to the loss and confusion you feel from not having one.

But there are many others who suffer from the self-same problem but who do not seek refuge in youth culture. Instead they look and act their age. But whether the profound sense of living an empty life hides behind a power suit or tweeds or a trendy top and frayed baggy jeans, what is underneath is always the same: a lost little boy or girl, desperate to find out who they are. The only way to do that is to explore the world – inner and outer – with a generous, attuned parental guide. Which is where, at our best, we therapists come in.

Suggested Resource

The Life Cycle Completed: A review by Erik Erikson (Norton)

Having a Happy Birthday

If your birthday is something to tolerate rather than celebrate, it may be time to invest more in the occasion.

I just had the most untypical birthday. The mythology about 'the big 4-0' demands that it is a time for serious soul-searching, and I was asked many times, especially at my eighties disco celebration, how I was handling the passing of this major milestone. Yet I just didn't feel it was very significant. In the spirit of 'physician, heal thyself', I thought I'd better undertake some self-analysis to check I wasn't in denial.

  I concluded that my particular life course meant that I had, indeed, escaped the turbulence traditionally associated with passing into one's fifth decade. My breakdown ten years ago, and subsequent retraining as a psychotherapist, allied to my late romantic development and its accompanying recent marriage and fatherhood, means that both professionally and personally I feel, in large part, that I am at the start of my life, as opposed to halfway through it.

I began to say all this in response to those who asked me how I was coping with turning 40. It made sense to them, though one wise friend added mischievously 'Well, let's see what happens at 50.' His quip revealed the truth that, wherever we are on our life's trajectory, birthdays at some point will trigger personal crises of confidence. That is why, as we get older, more and more of us see birthdays as something to tolerate rather than celebrate. They focus our minds less on what we've achieved and more on what we've not.

Accordingly we belittle these most personal anniversaries to ourselves and those around us. Some people actually let the day go by without remark; others demand no fuss is made. Most of us seem to find it hard to accept the world's spotlight on us at this time, as we fear the inevitable consequence: that we also shine a light on ourselves.

But rather than shrug off these annual alarm calls, we would be better served facing up to their full meaning in all their glory. We should, consciously and actively, celebrate our birth and what we have achieved so far in life, even if we feel our major success has been surviving. We should set aside time to remember our parents (I think we forget that our birthdays are actually as significant for our mothers as for us), the child we were, the teenager we became and all the ups and downs since.

We should also actively and specifically analyse where we are and what we want to change before next year. Obviously this may not be something you want to do at your actual party, but try and set aside an hour or two in the days beforehand. Jot down some ideas and make some plans. Get in touch with your regrets, fears and hopes. Bringing these to the surface won't overshadow your subsequent celebration, they will make it seem more grounded and real.

If you are shuddering at these ideas and have a small voice querying, 'Why? Why do we have to do these things?' the answer is very simple. Our birthdays, as their name suggests, stir up deep within us the idea of life. If we cannot face – and embrace – these relatively rare days of remembrance and renewal, then we are, on a fundamental level, turning away from life.

Each passing birthday takes us closer, chronologically, to our death. That is why, every year, we must invest the awareness and commitment necessary to assert, in the face of this unchallengeable truth, that we remain on the side of life. Not tolerating it, but celebrating it. So, happy birthday to me!

Suggested Resources

The Seasons of a Man's Life by Daniel Levinson (Ballantine Books)
The Seasons of a Woman's Life by Daniel Levinson (Ballantine Books)

Dreaming On

When we sleep our minds come alive, but what do our nocturnal musings really mean? At the very least, your dreams may reveal some surprising connections.

Almost always, if I am seeing someone for psychotherapy over many months, they will start to tell me about their dreams. Not because I have initiated such explorations, it just seems that, after a while, people find it natural to begin sharing their nocturnal visions, assuming that these must have some meaning. But in the world of psychology there is a terrific debate about whether they are right.

On the one hand the Freudians and Jungians believe that interpreting our dreams can reveal what we unconsciously want or believe. Freud went as far as to call dreaming 'the royal road to the unconscious'. Ranged against these two are the neuroscientists who argue that the years of our lives we spend dreaming are just the result of random electrical impulses, travelling from one part of the brain to another without rhyme or reason.

Other researchers believe that dreams are meaningless, but nonetheless vital: they process unexpressed emotions built up during the day, 'clearing out' the brain for the trials and tribulations of tomorrow. You may have wanted to punch your boss, but wisely restrained yourself; hours later, when you are safely tucked up in bed, you dream of a volcano erupting and spewing out awesome destruction.

Despite hundreds of studies, books and papers, we don't know, scientifically, who is right. Luckily I don't think it matters. Either in the consulting room, or as we lie in bed trying to piece together the dreams we've just woken up from, whether our dreams hold a particular key to what's on our unconscious mind isn't the most important question. Let me explain.

Freud believed that the interpretation of dreams (which was the title of his first great book, published in 1901) depended on 'association'. He broke down his own dreams to reveal their meaning, and concluded that each object, event or idea stands for something else.

His approach was intuitive and subtle, but such a process can lead to reductive 'dream dictionaries' where snakes = penises. One online dream dictionary asserts that almonds = wealth and cabbages = a poor property deal. Whether transparently ridiculous or plausible, these pat associations throw us off the scent because they suggest what objects *should* symbolize, in the eye of the author, not what they actually symbolize to us.

So don't look up your dream. Find a quiet moment

and do some associating of your own. If you dreamt of a fire engine rushing to an emergency, say, ask yourself: what comes to mind when I think of that fire engine? It might be something obvious such as 'danger', but maybe what springs to mind is the fair you went to as a youngster, where the fire brigade put on an exciting display.

In the dream maybe the fire engine then rotted away and turned to rust. What does rust remind you of? Let's suppose it's your dad's tools lying idly in the garage since he's been ill. Then you remember it was your dad who took you to that fondly remembered fairground. Suddenly you remember how much you've meant to go and visit him, and that you keep putting it off. You make plans to go at the weekend.

Now, you may think all this is far-fetched. Certainly, some scientists would say that the whole thing is nonsense, searching for meaning where none exists. But as I said earlier, I don't think it matters – because the important bit comes not with the dream itself but with the associating.

In this instance, the fire engine allowed a chain of thoughts to emerge that was previously buried: an aware-ness of guilt and the need to take some action. It is what we reach for when we start to analyse our dreams that matters. Maybe their content is an ingenious key that guides us to inevitable and unique conclusions. Or maybe the fire engine is a false alarm – no more than a convenient prop that lets us leap imaginatively to where our minds already want to go. I suspect it is a mixture of the two.

Until we find out for sure, if we ever do, let's keep dreaming, and analysing, and see where it takes us. If we end up somewhere that rings true, then we've learned something. If not, there's always tonight.

Suggested Resource

The Interpretation of Dreams by Sigmund Freud (The Hogarth Press)

Dealing with the Past

Unhappy events from our past have a lasting effect on our lives, boiling up when we least expect them. But we can break free by getting to the root of these feelings.

I am lucky enough to have supervision with renowned therapist Susie Orbach. Supervision is standard practice for therapists, and involves discussing the more difficult issues thrown up by your patients with a more experienced colleague. It's not supposed to be therapy, but we spend a few minutes at the beginning of our meeting having a general catch-up.

A while back I had written an article about Tony Blair. I mentioned to Susie that I was highly critical of him, and had surprised myself with the depth of my hostility, especially as I had worked for New Labour in its early days. She acknowledged that this was no doubt partly about politics but asked, perceptively, if anything else might be going on. 'What does Tony Blair mean to you?' she asked.

She was getting at something that can lie behind many disagreements, feuds and conflicts, and consume massive amounts of our time and energy: sometimes we think we are fighting so-and-so but actually, unknown to us, we are actually at war with someone – or something – completely different.

Take the example of Ted. He would get into all sorts of arguments with traffic wardens, council officials and the like. These usually involved ranting and raving but could also escalate to incidents where the police would be called, or to drawn-out and expensive court cases.

I am sure he did sometimes have cause for complaint, but when we posed the question, 'What do these bureaucrats mean to you?' we discovered that they reminded him of his stepdad, a weak but spiteful man who had attempted to control and constrain Ted throughout his childhood with petty rules and arbitrary decisions. When we explored Ted's anger at the unfairness of this, and the grief at losing his dad that lay buried underneath, he found that the rage subsided and he could much more easily brush off frustrating encounters. He was now conscious that they were triggering off something else entirely.

Similarly, Alice suffered from a powerful pull to row and feud with her younger sister. This made family gatherings unpleasant and left Alice feeling miserable and guilty. There were things about her sister that genuinely annoyed her, but when we asked the question, 'What does your sister mean to you?' we discovered that a much deeper issue lay behind her hostility.

When Alice was a little girl her newborn sister had been very ill and her mum had spent many days in hospital and became distracted and worried. Unbeknownst to the adult Alice, her child's mind had deduced from this that Alice's mum preferred her sister. When the family were together, any interest from their mum in Alice's sister would trigger these fears and Alice would pick a fight. After exploring all this in therapy Alice disconnected her childhood fantasies from adult reality and relations between the sisters improved enormously.

So, if you find yourself in a similar cycle of conflict, try and step aside from it for a moment and ask yourself that question: what does this person (or thing) mean to me? You may not need to talk it through with a therapist. A good, unbiased friend might provide an adequate sounding board. Or just pondering it and seeing what comes into your mind can throw up insights. Some people find that writing down their thoughts and feelings, either in a journal or just on a piece of paper, can stimulate greater understanding of why we do what we do.

Almost always, such negative dynamics are unproductive and make us feel bad. But we can break free of them when we separate out the trigger from what it unconsciously reminds us of. As for me and Tony Blair, I'm still musing over what he means to me, and why I felt quite so much antagonism towards him. It's taking me a while to figure it out. Hey, I never said it was easy.

Suggested Resource

No One Is to Blame by Robert Hoffman (Hoffman Institute)

Being Too Dependent

A reliance on a certain pattern of behaviour – smoking, casual sex, shopping – usually masks feelings of low self-esteem. But it is possible to move out of your comfort zone.

One of the worries people often have about entering therapy is that they'll become 'dependent'. That's always a tricky one for us therapists, as dependency isn't always a bad thing. Feeling comfortable with being dependent is a prerequisite to being able to be independent, and outside the consulting room we can become dependent on all sorts of things – people, objects, activities. The stuff we rely on becomes a sort of furniture that defines the shape of our lives. And there's nothing wrong with having rhythms and routines in one's life.

The problem is that we can become too dependent on our dependences. You see, I don't believe that there are clear dividing lines between habits, obsessions and addictions. In reality, these are all points on a continuum. How, then, do you know if your dependence is healthy or not? And what do you do about it if it isn't?

There is a straightforward assessment you can apply, which I call the 3D test: how damaging, distracting or dominant is the dependence?

The first question requires stepping back from the comfort you get from the activity and honestly evaluating its cost. The classic example would be smoking. For all it might give you, the potential damage is too high. Other activities, like out-of-control shopping, constantly checking your BlackBerry or whatever, also carry a price. Sometimes habit means that we just 'get used' to our high debt or inability to relax. See if you can identify the costs involved and try and keep them at the front – not the back – of your mind.

But the allure of our idiosyncrasies can be very strong, and this is often because of the second factor you should examine: their role in distracting you. Obviously some relief from responsibility and worry is a good thing. As ever, with our emotional health, it comes down to a question of balance. Often we use our more compulsive behaviours to chase away feelings we don't want to have. If we keep texting our friends, it can be because then we won't have to think about feeling too lonely. If we concentrate on wearing exactly the right outfit, and shopping to buy it, we know we won't be so in touch with the fact that we've been feeling a bit down recently.

So find out what happens when you stop for a while. If unwelcome emotions come up during a period of abstinence, don't reach for the old habit to chase them away, but allow them to surface and try to work them through. Maybe it would be better to arrange to spend quality time with a friend you miss, rather than sending out a dozen texts. Maybe going through a bit of introspection will prove more life-changing than the latest outfit.

If you find the compulsion to take up your crutch again is irresistible, then you may need help – not because the specific activity you're indulging in is necessarily harmful in itself, but because there could be something serious underneath that you're too desperate to avoid.

The third test you can apply to your dependences relates to their dominance in your life. Does one particular activity – or all our little dependences added up together – trap us in a way of living that precludes experimentation? We can get so accustomed to our habits that we become extremely reluctant to break out of our comfort zone and try something else. So if you feel that the majority of what you do is predetermined by habit, make a conscious effort to do something completely different this weekend.

If you're lost for inspiration, try and remember what used to excite you as a child. If you loved kite-flying, get a kite and go out to the park. If you loved the fairground, get some friends together and go to the nearest theme park. If curling up with a novel was what absorbed your teenage self, visit the local library or bookshop, turn off the mobile and enjoy a good read.

Our dependences can be some of the best friends we have: reliable, pleasurable and comforting. But they can also turn, without us realizing it, into seducers or bullies, forcing us away from what might be better for us. So maybe it's time to give your dependences the 3D test. Are they TOO damaging? TOO distracting? TOO dominant? If they are, then it's time to try going without.

Suggested Resource

The Addictive Personality: Understanding the Addictive Process and Compulsive Behavior by Craig Nakken (Hazelden)

Getting Addicted

You don't need drugs or alcohol to get you through the day, so you think you don't have a problem? Think again. Harmful stimulants come in many forms.

We all think we know what an addict looks like, don't we? Hollow eyes, dirty clothes, f***ed-up life, right? But how about sparkling persona, designer suit, fantastic social life? How about looking more closely at the person working across from you? Or the guest sitting next to you at dinner? Or how about looking in the mirror?

There are many different degrees of addiction, and some are less obvious than others. One of the devices we use to tell ourselves we're fine is to paint a picture of a junkie who seems a million miles away from us – what Carl Jung called 'the other'. Jung's 'the other' is reassuringly alien to our own self-image – and this is precisely why we are so attached to the idea of it. But, according to Jung, that 'other' can in fact be cunningly concealed within us.

In my consulting room I often see high-functioning people who look as unlike our image of the out-of-control addict as it is possible to be. Yet some hold their lives together around a private obsession – be it snorting coke almost every single day, spending all weekend internet gambling, or downing two bottles of wine a night. These secret, full-blown addictions are more common than people realize. Even these, though, are still relatively rare. A far more widespread condition, that afflicts millions of us, is what I call 'stimulant addiction' – the pernicious product of a modern stimulant society.

Take the marketing manager who gets coked up at weekends. Along with most of his mates, he finds himself in the pub after work nearly every night, and if he does get home before midnight, he paces around fidgeting until he puts on some DVD porn, or kills a few hours on his PlayStation.

Or consider the human resources executive who spends her lunch breaks and weekends maxing out credit cards on designer clothes, and always has a bottle of wine on the go at home. When she isn't boozing or shopping, she's compulsively checking for a text from her on–off boyfriend, or re-reading emails the 'love-of-her-life' sent her three years ago.

Neither of these types is a classic junkie. But in a sense, they might as well be. What they both share is the junkie's compulsion to fill every minute with intoxicating, thrilling distractions. And today's society caters wonderfully to the stimulant junkie's desires, feeding their habit with limitless consumer diversions – internet porn, 24-hour gyms, instant messaging and that über-compulsion of modern life – overwork.

The heroin addict does at least know he or she has a problem. The stimulant addict is often unaware that anything is even wrong, for modern society condones – even celebrates – the tireless, hard-working party animal with the fabulously up-to-date wardrobe. But the desire to lead such a stimulant-enriched lifestyle comes, I believe, from exactly the same emotional source as heroin addiction or life-shattering alcoholism – a desperate, overwhelming need to fill an emotional and spiritual void.

If any of this sounds familiar to you, turn off your mobile and television for a minute, and write down all the frenetic devices you think you might use to fill up your day. Then, for the next 48 hours, try to live without them. If you manage to do it, and feel better for it, you may have the strength within yourself to re-balance your life and find some space to just 'be'. After all, some people do manage to give up drink or cigarettes or even illegal drugs, with nothing more than simple willpower.

But if you have really struggled with your 48-hour abstinence, you may need help. You will probably find that some very unpleasant feelings – loneliness, depression or anxiety – come bubbling up to the surface. That is to be expected. They are the very feelings that all that manic stimulation is designed to mask. As yet there are no 12-step meetings for stimulant junkies, so you will probably need to find a therapist to help you.

Why bother, you might ask? Non-stop stimulation can be fun. But it is also dangerous. The stimulant lifestyle makes it difficult to develop meaningful romantic relationships, and even harder to provide children with the stability and groundedness they need. And, in the end, a frantic lifestyle will always take its toll. No matter how busy you keep yourself, underlying depression, anxiety or panic attacks will break through.

But there is a bigger reason – one which is more important than all of these. While the stimulant craver is busy chasing the next exciting distraction, the real you is left behind somewhere else, often suffering in silence. When we see the archetypal addict, we usually think of a life being tragically wasted. That junkie is not alone.

Suggested Resource

The Heart of Addiction by Lance Dodes (HarperCollins)

Techno-stress

What it is and what to do about it.

There are some therapists who remain steadfastly old-fash-
ioned when it comes to client contact, never giving out their
mobile numbers or using email. They check in with their office answerphones regularly and that is as hi-tech as it gets.
Others, like me, are happy to be more contactable, though
we run the risk of that access being exploited. Luckily that
rarely happens and clients are respectful of the fact that
therapists need not to be on call 24/7.

But there is a good reason, apart from the occasional
emergency, for therapists to use all the usual modern ways
of communicating. I think, whenever we can, we need to
show that we are just like our clients: living in the same
world with the same pressures. We may question these
more, and keep sessions themselves as an oasis of a different, calmer sort of space, but I don't think it helps for us to
appear 'otherworldly'.

The reality is that life today involves unprecedented pressure. The average office worker has to respond to phone

calls, mobile calls, texts, email and probably personal email too. All this may come in one handy hand-held device, but that just makes the chaos more 'convenient'. Many people don't keep up and therapists are getting used to treating stress that is related to overloaded in-boxes, ever-increasing working hours and a sense of drowning in data, messages and tasks.

It's not easy, though. You can't tell your client to step off the treadmill. Job, promotion, mortgage and pension plans all rest on the ability to keep up. This frantic lifestyle has been critiqued by Oliver James in his recent book *Affluenza* and he recommends nothing less than a revolution whereby we give up our obsession with money, consumerism and status. That, though, for most of us, isn't likely to happen anytime soon. So what can we do?

If therapists simply respond by listening sympathetically and exploring better ways of coping, through skills such as prioritizing, delegating and the like, then I think they do their clients a disservice. Because, while much of this pressure comes from the world outside, some of it comes, unwittingly, from ourselves, and that is something we have got control over, at least in theory.

What I find when I explore all this with clients is that a lot of their techno-stress is self-inflicted. One of my patients is busy enough, but if her BlackBerry does fall silent for a minute she is prodding it, sending off messages that aren't really necessary or responding to messages she could let slide. If all else fails, she sends Facebook or YouTube jokes to

friends – anything to keep busy. She is the one keeping up the pressure, if her work ever does let up.

When we explored this, using a visualization in which she disconnected from all her gadgets, we discovered that being 'out of touch' provoked a low-level anxiety. She felt, as she put it, 'antsy'. This turned out to be about worries she was blocking out with all her techno-activity. Her recourse to it was playing precisely the same – if less extreme – role that alcohol or drugs provide to an addict: distracting her from things she didn't want to think about.

Once we had started to address these, her need to 'keep busy' decreased and she was able to enjoy those rare moments when the outside world was not making demands. It often still did, and her stress continues at too high a level, but she is no longer contributing to it. She has kicked her habit and learned to disconnect when circumstances allow.

Because the amount of information and requests we are bombarded with is so great it is easy to blame 'the office' or 'the modern world', and that is a big part of the story. But by doing so we neglect our own part in our stressed-up downfall. If we make room for the idea that all that pressure may also be serving a purpose for us, and begin to explore what that may be, we open up the chance of being able to switch off – at least for a while.

Suggested Resource

The Power of Now by Eckhart Tolle (Hodder & Stoughton)

Avoiding Depression

Whether you're depressed or just unhappy, you don't have to accept things the way they are. An understanding of your mood can help clear those dark clouds.

I am occasionally a guest on Radio 2's *Jeremy Vine Show*. On one show the subject under discussion was, 'Does counselling work?' The calls and emails that came in, and those that I have received since, indicate that the vast majority of people believe it does.

But the feedback also revealed that many people wrestle with a different question: not whether therapy would work for them, but whether they need it. I think this is especially true when it comes to depression. How do you know whether it's 'clinical' or just the blues?

There's been a lot of discussion recently about happiness, with happiness classes planned for state school pupils, and the seminal book *Happiness* by Professor Richard Layard influencing policy at the very top of the government. David Cameron has joined in, saying once that as well as

paying attention to our GDP (Gross Domestic Product), we should also be trying to increase our GWB – General Well-Being.

In therapy, though, I don't find the concept of 'happiness' particularly useful. I think that the related but subtly different ideas of 'contentment' and 'joy' provide better yardsticks about how we're doing emotionally and whether we might need help.

Happiness seems too definite a state. In reality, however psychologically healthy we are, we'll be experiencing a mix of emotions. All of us go through bad patches when life seems a struggle. It may be because of what psychologists call 'situational stressors' such as illness, a bereavement, a relationship break-up or a challenging time at work. Or it may be that we are going through a fallow period, or perhaps a transition into young adulthood or middle-age.

But no matter how difficult life is, and how unhappy we feel, if we are fundamentally emotionally healthy we will still have times when we feel content. Time spent with friends or indulging in a favourite pastime, or just a sunny day, could bring it out in us. We temporarily forget our cares. We feel – and it is a physical sensation as much as a mental one – calm, centred and content.

Also, no matter how miserable we are, if things are essentially OK we will, even if only fleetingly, feel the odd moment of unadulterated joy – triggered by, say, a particular piece of news, or something we see unexpectedly that's beautiful or funny, or someone touching us with their concern or love.

That leads us to a simple but effective test for depression. For it is the absolute absence of these two states — contentment and joy — that indicate, I believe, that you are suffering from something more profound than unhappiness. Unhappiness should eventually sort itself out (though it may take a lot of time and work), but if the memory of even passing contentment or joy seems very far away, or if it's hard to remember what either even feels like, then it may be that you are suffering from a clinical depression — and should consider seeking treatment.

You may well be resistant to the idea that you are suffering in this way. Many people experience shame that depression could happen to them. Often they feel guilty because life 'should' be good, even though the outward trappings of success don't make them feel any better.

Unhappiness can be pictured as an overcast sky. Sometimes the clouds part and a burst of sunshine appears. Depression, on the other hand, is like a blanket of cloudy, grey sky. The sun, for all we see of it, may as well have died.

One of Jeremy Vine's callers said that without treatment for her depression she wouldn't have been alive. She didn't just mean she might have killed herself; she meant that how she had been living under her grey skies didn't merit being called a life.

But here's the good news. Depression can be treated, most effectively with a mixture of antidepressants and therapy. If you are beset by clouds, do not despair: it may be hard to believe, but behind them your own personal sun is still shining, waiting to burst through.

Suggested Resources

Authentic Happiness by Martin E. P. Seligman (Nicholas Brealey Publishing Ltd)

Feeling Good by David D. Burns (Avon Books)

Accepting Unhappiness

We need to acknowledge our fears before things can begin to get better.

During difficult times, we often hear alarming stories on the news about house-price crashes and economic downturns. The anxiety these kinds of things cause has come up more than once in my consulting room. It's difficult to respond to this grey outlook with anything but gloom, but does this mean we're all going to be plunged into depression? And if we are, is it something therapists should be trying to do something about?

The movement known as 'positive psychology' sets out explicitly to make people happier, using the latest scientific evidence. It has been the most popular course at Harvard University for several years and is now being taught at Wellington College and, as a pilot, in some state schools in the UK.

Some therapists, though, are wary of this lofty ambition and like to aim lower, offering only to help clients 'understand themselves better'. Indeed, the grandfather of psychotherapy, Sigmund Freud, famously declared, 'The aim of psychoanalysis is to turn neurotic misery into ordinary human unhappiness.'

Now, I've been studying Freud for years and the old man had a wily sense of humour. He would often exaggerate to make a point, and I suspect he was doing so here. However, there is an insight contained within his rhetoric. For although people, of course, and rightly, come to therapy in order to find happiness, I often think the road to it depends on first helping clients give themselves permission to feel miserable.

One man came to see me nearly a year after his treatment had ended. It had been reasonably successful: he had stopped having panic attacks, was less depressed and more able to be there for his young daughter. He looked, by the end, a physically different person, more relaxed, attractive and somehow 'lighter'.

Yet here he was, ten months later, explaining that he felt absolutely awful. It turned out that his ex-wife was harassing both him and their child to the extent that the police had been involved. His new relationship had broken up, partly because of his ex's behaviour. On top of this, his dad was dying of cancer.

I took a deep breath. 'It is right, and healthy, for you to be feeling so miserable. Things have been terrible, and it's not over.' He started to cry, and after a bit I could finally hear his words through the sobs. He was saying 'Thank you.' He felt such relief at being given permission to feel bad.

If you've gone through a depression, any passing dark cloud raises the fear that you are having a relapse. Depression, as Professor Lewis Wolpert said, is only sadness's malignant twin. But the two *are* different.

Despite our populist use of the term, 'depression' in the clinical sense is not a passing blue mood. In fact, its defining characteristic is that it *doesn't* pass. It stays, no matter what the outside weather. This distinction is a crucial one to grasp if we want to navigate the storm of our feelings successfully.

Therapy – and indeed, emotional health – is not about feeling 'good'; it is about feeling what is appropriate. Sometimes our emotions get way out of whack, as in a clinical depression. But much of the time grief, misery, fear and anger are the authentic responses to what life has thrown at us. We need to feel the pain and, eventually, although it never feels like this at the time, things will get better.

Even if we are in an economic depression, we needn't feel depressed. Worried, bitter, fearful, angry, sad – yes. Just like the economy, our feelings inevitably run in cycles, and the flipside of the good times are the bad times. No therapist can make those completely go away, nor should they try. All any of us can do is let the feelings in, and hope for the upturn.

Suggested Resource

Finding Hope in the Age of Melancholy by David S. Awbrey (Little Brown)

Being Your Own Worst Enemy?

If you seem intent on self-destruction, maybe you are dancing to someone else's tune. If you discover whose, you can change the record.

It always amazes me how many clichés prove perfectly apt for the consulting room. It is no good just dishing them out, though. Obviously patients expect more than to be told 'When in a hole, stop digging' or 'Better to see the glass as half full'. I guess this just goes to show why they have become clichés – they speak to those all-too-common moments when, as human beings, 'we can't see the wood for the trees'.

The cliché that probably applies more than any other in therapy, though, is one that is very difficult to raise, either in its hackneyed form or in a more personalized version. In many therapies, even after we have analysed the root causes of someone's issues, and worked on tools and skills to help them change their behaviour, they still seem stuck. At that point I often find myself wanting to say, 'But you are your own worst enemy!'

For there comes a time, in everyone's therapeutic journey, when the past has to be left behind. We have uncovered childhood pain and learned to accept it, we have identified patterns that hold us back; now we need to take that vital last step of doing things differently.

Take a man I have seen for a couple of years. He grew up in an incredibly sterile home. His mum lived in a mild alcoholic stupor. Most of the time she wasn't really there, other times she would be the typical mawkish drunk, invading his space and crying about how much she loved him. His dad was no help; he was either at work or shut away working on his hobby of making models.

Outwardly successful, deep down my patient felt miserable and lonely, and was incapable of getting close to women. He covered this up by working all hours, seducing a string of ever-younger girls and visiting lap-dance clubs.

We started by facing up to the pain of his childhood and discovered that the loneliness he felt today was really the loneliness he'd experienced, year after year, as a child. We linked this to his current avoidance of intimacy and sexual promiscuity – he was seeking fleeting sensation because he just wasn't used to really being close to someone. If someone did come close he felt invaded and suffocated. It was the seesaw of his mother's abandonment and encroachment.

With these insights he was able to give up his excessive behaviour and began to date women in a more normal way. But still, whenever things got too close he would end up drunk in a strip club trying — and sometimes succeeding — to persuade one of the strippers to go home with him. As this destructive behaviour went on I began to get frustrated. I had done what I could, and now it was down to him. Couldn't he see what he was doing?

Then we had a breakthrough.

After another such episode he was talking about the girl he'd picked up, and mumbled, 'She doesn't want me to be happy.' When we explored this we realized that he hadn't been talking about the girl but about his mother, now long dead. Deep down he believed that his mother (or the memory of her inside him) resented his attempts to grow up and settle down. That, somehow, if he succeeded at this, he would be finally leaving her behind. His inability to be happy was, in the final analysis, the only bond they had – his misery echoing hers.

So we discovered that, actually, he wasn't his own worst enemy. What appeared to be his failure was actually the powerful presence of his mother — willing him to fail, and using unconscious emotional blackmail to ensure he did.

Once he understood this, he was able to break free and really get his act together. It made me realize that whenever — in therapy or outside it — we think someone is the wilful architect of their own destruction, the more likely explanation is that, without realizing it, they are dancing to someone else's tune.

Suggested Resource

You Can Change Your Life by Tim Laurence (Mobius)

Crying Shame

Many of us try to cover up the feelings of shame we carry with us, but burying these emotions can cause long-term problems. We need to face up to them.

When I trained as a therapist in California I worked a lot with troubled children and adolescents. Often they would find it hard to express their emotions, but I discovered that they didn't just have a problem with 'letting it out', they often didn't know what they were feeling in the first place. So I used a sheet with dozens of emotions written on it – such as happiness, anger, fear – and would ask them to choose the one that best fitted what they were experiencing, and we'd discuss what that feeling was all about.

Sadly it's not just kids who have difficulty identifying their emotional state. Often adults struggle to name their feelings, too. So occasionally, and always slightly wary that I'll be seen as patronizing, I hand out that same sheet today. Almost always it's helpful, and the range of emotions, and the different words we have for our feelings, often surprise people.

There is one feeling, though, that consistently causes puzzlement in people. Most of us don't have a clear grasp of what it really is. Yet it is at the root of many people's unhappiness and discomfort with themselves. That feeling is shame.

Shame is most often confused with embarrassment or guilt, but these relate to feeling bad about something you've done. Shame is feeling bad about who you are. We can do something about our guilt or embarrassment: apologize, make amends, start behaving differently. If we feel deep shame about ourselves it seems there is nothing we can do, because no matter what good we 'do', that can never wipe out the badness that we 'are'.

This often emerges in the consulting room with women who constantly play a role with men, never letting their partners see the real them. This is very hard to maintain in a consistent way, and many women's apparent 'high maintenance' and mood swings are actually the results of trying to keep this role going, rather than something that is intrinsic to who they really are.

Even if they can keep it up, the men in their lives often sense their fundamental falseness and quickly move on. On analysing this phenomenon, time and time again I have heard them eventually say, 'But if he got to know the real me, he wouldn't like me.' When I scratch beneath the surface they go further – that others would detest or be disgusted by the real them.

It is that word 'disgust' that is the clue. It is shame's emotional mirror. Yet these are invariably attractive, kind, smart women. They don't hold hidden horrors other than their terrible shame at just being themselves.

This sense of being worthless stems, often, from a lack of being appreciated for who they really were when they were children. Unfortunately, peer group and societal and cultural pressure to look and act a certain way can exacerbate this. I have known women who have grown up pretending to be the person they think others want them to be every minute of every day, and only when they are alone do they, sometimes just fleetingly, get a glimpse of the empty desolation at their core. They then conclude, falsely, that this makes them somehow broken or bad people. It actually just means that they have never been seen, understood or appreciated for who they really are, not least by themselves.

Recovering from these levels of what is sometimes called 'toxic shame' is hard. It first involves people recognizing the good parts of themselves – not the people-pleasing act, but what lies underneath. There's then a huge amount of pain unleashed when they recognize that they have lived this way for so long, and been so cruel and dismissive of themselves.

Then there needs to be an acceptance that they, like all of us, have their bad parts. That they are not perfect, as their performances demand they be. That it's normal to sometimes dislike yourself, be ashamed and feel damaged. But that these should not be the core of one's being. And that feelings of love, pride and joy are just as valid, and hopefully increasingly able to be found.

Many people don't even begin this process of recovery. They live all their life as balls of self-loathing and shame, covered up by a more 'acceptable' persona. Others slide into a life of self-abuse: drug taking, unhealthy living and promiscuity that is designed to confirm and personify their internal shame, because they can't imagine an alternative.

They should know that the alternative is there, though it is a painful, long and difficult journey. It is an honour, as a therapist, to help someone along the way. But it still sometimes chills me that people can need to do so much just to end up simply feeling OK.

Suggested Resource

Healing the Shame that Binds You by John Bradshaw (Health Communications)

Making a Change

We may think that we can change, but occasionally we just have to accept that there are some things we can't get over. That's no cause for alarm.

When I first worked in politics, I knew a wise old Labour lord called Michael Montague. I still remember one of his favourite sayings: 'You can change people,' he would say with a twinkle in his eyes, then pause before going on, '... by five per cent for five minutes'.

It was, of course, an unduly cynical mantra, but one that made sense in the Westminster jungle, where people are always trying to pretend to be something they are not. But I have often pondered his words as I plough my new furrow in the world of psychotherapy. Is he right? Is change so hard?

My own experience tells me he's wrong. I no longer crave drugs and promiscuity. Neither do I any longer slump into debilitating depressions. My life has changed – if I had to put a figure on it, probably by about 75 per cent for at least the last five years, and counting.

I also see change in my patients. It can be quick or take a long time. Often some movement takes place straightaway, and that can provide great relief, but we often then go on to hit a bedrock of deep, character-based difficulties that only time and hard work will heal. Indeed, my own five years of wellbeing came after about five years of therapy.

Sometimes, however, change *isn't* possible. When someone fails to make progress in therapy it can provoke a lot of soul-searching on the part of the therapist. Did I fail? Let them down? Am I really cut out for this work? Sometimes the temptation is to frame the failure more positively: 'The patient got a glimpse of the work that needs doing; they'll return to therapy when the time is right.' It is better to live with the truth: that it's often impossible to tell why the therapy didn't work, and that the failure is a sad, uncomfortable event that has to be borne, not rationalized away.

That approach suggests a model of how we can live with other unpalatable events and aspects of ourselves. One of my favourite quotes comes from the great analyst Donald Winnicott. A woman wrote to him pleading for help after her little toddler died. She was distraught and desperate to know what to do. He wrote back a short, handwritten note. 'I am so sorry, I cannot help. This is a disaster.'

I don't know how she took that, but I like to imagine she felt some relief. Sometimes we have to face up to the terrible fact that we can't fix certain things. The wonder of good therapy is that it can give us the chance to try, but it should also be a place where we can admit failure, as patients and as therapists. I'd like to say that such an admission, in itself, is therapeutic in some way, but I am falling into the trap I have just described.

The best formulation for how to deal with all this can be found in the 12-step movement, although it was originally a German Christian prayer from the 1930s: 'God grant me the serenity to accept the things I cannot change, the courage to change the things I can, and the wisdom to know the difference.'

I like to think that wily old Lord Montague, who tragically died of a heart attack in the House of Lords itself weeks after taking up his peerage, was aiming his words at those who haven't mastered this distinction. I have concluded that he was therefore half-right. But I prefer the idea that we can change – maybe not by 95 per cent, but certainly in real and lasting ways. But we need to be ready to acknowledge when it's not possible. That then requires working on stuff even more challenging than change: grief, loss and acceptance.

Suggested Resource

Attachment and Loss by John Bowlby (Pimlico)

PART 2

UNDERSTANDING YOUR RELATIONSHIPS

Falling in Love

We may think it's all about fate or blinding chemistry, but the reasons we fall in love often have more to do with attempting to compensate for what we lack.

Many people coming for therapy are seeking help with finding love. Often they have a track record of failed relationships and 'bad choices' that seem inexplicable. I can't fail to sympathize, as I too spent many years in relationships that were ultimately unfulfilling and seemed to make no sense.

When I first started therapy, my therapist, after just a few sessions, spotted this pattern and gave me a book which years later I often find myself recommending to my patients. Entitled *Understanding the Psychology of Romantic Love*, it provocatively labels romantic love a myth. It doesn't solve all love's mysteries, or even try to, but it does highlight one deeply ingrained myth at the heart of our culture: that if only we find the 'right' person, then we will feel complete.

Although we might feel that the person we fall in love with, and why we fall for them, are unfathomable, there is all too often a method to our madness. For when we think we are searching for that special something in someone else, we are often looking for something very different: a missing part of ourselves.

One patient of mine was very controlling – in a low-key, benign, but nonetheless pervasive way. After several months in therapy we had identified and recognized this. The great love of her life had been a dominant, sometimes cruel man whom she nonetheless felt enthralled by. She talked of 'surrendering' to him.

What she was actually surrendering, we came to understand, was her need to always be in control and the exhaustion that went with it. As she learned to relax this need, she could give up her continuing obsession with her ex. She reclaimed the part of her that didn't have to be in control all the time, and as she integrated that with the other parts of her, she didn't need to hand it over lock, stock and barrel to someone else.

The tricky part is that usually, as was the case here, the whole process is unconscious – we don't know why we do what we do. So actually, though you may believe you always choose the wrong man, on one level you are choosing the *right* man. You just aren't aware of the gap he is filling. Which is precisely what makes him so compelling, no matter how much accompanying dissatisfaction and drama there might be.

This seeking – and often finding – missing parts of yourself can take many forms. A promiscuous man might demand what seems like unreasonable fidelity from his partner, but actually he is seeking the faithful part of himself. An unassertive woman could find herself being constantly drawn to men who are successful and decisive, but what she really needs to do is discover and nurture the more self-confident parts of herself.

Of course, finding your missing capacities in someone else can be massively relieving, and allow you to glow in that pseudo-spiritual state of being 'truly madly deeply' in love, but as time goes by reality begins to set in. The rest of your beloved's personality comes to the fore and you find that maybe they are not such a match for your missing bit after all. Or, inevitably, that when the heat of passion dies away, you are left back where you started, still missing that essential element of yourself that should be part of you, on the inside, not projected out onto someone else.

For a relationship to work in the long term, and at a deep level, it has to be as free from these projections as possible. They will never be completely absent, nor should they be. Part of the mystery of love must be that we do find ourselves, sometimes, in the ones we love – but only in passing, and only fleetingly.

If we depend on someone else to feel whole, and without them feel something vital is missing from our very being, we are indulging in a fantasy – a thrilling, romantic, all-consuming fantasy maybe, but one that dooms us to remain, in reality, incomplete. Furthermore, it's a fantasy that is always in grave danger of shattering.

Suggested Resource

We: Understanding the Psychology of Romantic Love by Robert A. Johnson (Harper & Row)

The Go-Between

Couples therapy can reveal surprising mistakes we make about each other.

It is a truism that marriages often don't make sense to the outside world. Within a marriage something particular, almost magical, takes place between the two people involved that doesn't boil down to shared interests or passion or anything else visible to the rest of us. Sometimes that alchemy forms bright, strong partnerships that endure all storms; other times, it undermines and corrodes, and misery and breakdown are the inevitable result.

That makes the job of a couples therapist a particularly tough one. Understanding just one other mind is hard enough, but with a couple you need to understand three things before any progress can be made: each partner's mind, and the strange, mystical thing they have created between them.

I don't do too much work with couples. Apart from the sterling work done by Relate and pioneers like the Tavistock Centre for Couples Relationships, couples therapy is pretty uncommon in the UK. This, in my view, is a great shame, because my experience is that, often, seemingly insurmountable problems are nothing of the sort. When communications lines are opened, and trust rebuilt, the old magic can return.

I once saw a young couple, Louise and John, who were close to splitting up. Their bickering seemed pretty inconsequential – the kind of stuff that in a good relationship just gets sorted out, or swept aside by the good stuff. After a few sessions we focused in on the fact that John had been out of steady work for a year or two. Various projects hadn't taken off and he had, effectively, been living off Louise.

He assumed she resented this, she swore she didn't but there seemed to be something more going on. In the end, a classic Freudian slip gave the game away. Louise, when having a go at John over something relatively minor – he'd forgotten someone's birthday – said, 'It's no way for a father to behave.' Now, she quickly corrected this slip and insisted, 'I meant husband.' But the couple were childless, and I asked what kind of father John thought Louise felt he would be.

'A useless one!' John spat out instantly. They both turned to each other, ignoring me. Louise was genuinely shocked, 'But I married you because I thought you'd be a great father, and still do.' 'Well, why won't you have a kid, then? Because I don't have a proper job!' It turned out that John was labouring under a massive misunderstanding. Louise had thought he didn't want the burden of a child until he had got himself back on his feet; John meanwhile, unbeknownst to Louise, had begun to feel that he'd rather like to be a stay-at-home dad while Louise pursued her career, which he knew she loved. Louise, once she heard this idea, immediately agreed it would be the best way for them to start a family.

The next week they told me they wouldn't be coming to therapy any more as they were trying for a baby and were really happy. 'What about all the rows?' I ventured. 'Oh! They're nothing,' they both replied.

Now, it isn't always that easy. Sometimes it takes months of work to get at the central miscommunication that lies behind a couple's tensions. But sometimes it is as clear as it was with Louise and John. If you and your partner seem stuck in a rut of argument and recrimination, try and find space to explore it properly. You can play what I call 'the assumptions game'. Over a candlelit dinner and a bottle of wine, each write down, on a piece of paper, the assumptions you are making about the other person: their wants and priorities. Then, compare what you've described. I'll make a small bet. Two out of three are probably wrong. If you get two right, you're on a pretty secure footing. If you get all three right, do the exercise again, as you must be missing something!

For all the mystical properties of a good relationship, like most things that seem as if they are miracles, a lot of hard work lies behind the trick. That is good news, because it means that if the magic has gone, we may rediscover it rather more easily than we might expect.

Suggested Resource

What's the State of Your Union? Instant Relationship Self-Diagnosis by Maurice Taylor and Seana McGee – www.newcouple.com

Being Popular

Being liked and accepted can feel like the measure of our success as a person. But we should look at why it matters so much to us.

I am writing this in a morning stolen from my visit to the Labour Party conference, and I am still smarting from a major rejection I suffered last night. Among the dozens of receptions and events held here, there is only one that is really worth going to: the swanky News International party, home to newspapers including the *Sun* and *The Times*. It is, accordingly, the only one with a strict door policy. Knowing this, I'd asked a friend who works at the company to add my name to the guest list. I also turned up with the daughter of the editor of the *News of the World*. All to no avail. The guy on the door said I wasn't on the list and I wasn't getting in. I glanced at the throng inside and felt that they were all looking at me. As I turned away I felt cast out and dejected, like a little boy at school who hadn't been accepted into the cool gang in the playground. Prior to that moment I'd been on a high. Attending Labour's annual conference scratches my political itch and I get to see old friends, indulge in a bit of media commentating and put the world to rights while drinking late into the night. In short, I feel popular. But suddenly, shut out of the party, I felt like a loser.

Deep down, even strong self-esteem can sometimes be a shaky thing. I think that's a sign of health. Always feeling invincible is a sign of narcissism that often masks serious weaknesses that eventually burst out, or comes at the expense of shutting out real relationships with others. The occasional bit of self-doubt is to be welcomed. Also, of course, responding to others' reactions to us helps us work out how we are doing. Feeling good is about what we feel on the inside, but that sense of confidence rightly dances a tango with the messages we get from outside. Getting that balance right – between inner self-worth and the world's view of you – is the key to emotional and psychological health. Too much of the first and we can become disconnected and arrogant, and shut-off to the views and needs of others. Too much of the latter and we are buffeted from one experience to the next with no sense of firm psychological foundation. Most of us feel socially confident much of the time, but a rejection like this can puncture our self-possession. At moments like this, we're confronted with the reality of how much it matters to us to be popular. Do we even understand what popularity is?

To stop ourselves swinging between highs and lows, we need to work out what we mean by it. Is it being seen at the

most glamorous parties, or is it having good friends around us? By this morning I had realized that the main reason I'd wanted to get into that party was to see an old friend. So, after a bit of sulking and self-questioning, I texted him and we had coffee together. I may not have felt – or looked – popular last night, but in the cold light of day I retain my self-belief and my good friends. They, in the end, are more important even than popularity. Mind you, I will be doing my damnedest to get into that party next year.

Suggested Resource

The Philosophy of Friendship by Mark Vernon (Palgrave Macmillan)

How Much to Share?

Though you may be aware of important and uncomfortable aspects of your past, think twice before you let the people involved – your parents or partner – in on the secret.

One of the most challenging – and potentially frustrating – things about therapy is that, often, the more progress you make, the more difficulties and dilemmas emerge. The consulting room, after all, is one place where you are unlikely to be advised to let sleeping dogs lie. Instead, the more apt cliché is often the one involving cans of worms.

The good news is that, usually, there is a limit to the number of things that need to be addressed. The trick is to explore deeply enough to discover all of them. Once there are no more hidden 'issues', then treatment tends to proceed speedily, and in the best therapies, in the end, everything does seem to tie together and you feel as if you are making a genuinely new start.

Even this, though, can leave one outstanding dilemma: how much of what you have discovered should you share with your loved ones? It reflects a wider question that has relevance to all our relationships: how much of what we think and feel on the inside do we have a duty to share with those on the outside?

Let's get the obvious (though no less difficult for that) extremes out of the way. If what you are keeping secret is harming or grievously misleading others, then that's almost certainly not acceptable. If, on the other hand, you feel that you have a responsibility to share everything, no matter what havoc you might cause, then that is also, I'm afraid, rather suspect.

Because we do have the right to some part of ourselves that we don't share. It isn't necessary to tell your husband that you have been occasionally fantasizing about someone else when you have sex. It won't help anyone to admit that you lost their precious present when you can easily replace it. You don't need to let your best friend know that her prized new flat seems dull and cramped to you.

Of course, most practical dilemmas fall between the two poles of the corrosively deceitful and the little white lie. The classic one is confessing to a brief fling that is now over. Others that come up in therapy often involve letting your parents know that they have somehow let you down. The standard advice in such circumstances is not to confess all if you are doing it more for yourself than the other person or people involved. But in reality it can be very hard to separate out your underlying motivations. I suggest an alternative test.

This test relies on recognizing that there is no easy way out of these conundrums. Keeping mum or letting it all out, each carries a price in terms of inner and outer turmoil. How do you decide which way to go? I would pass the decision over to the more intuitive part of our brains – what, in common parlance, would be called 'letting your heart decide' or 'going with your gut feeling'.

Find a quiet place, and try and relax. Close your eyes and picture a calm, pleasant scene. Breathe deeply. After a while, bring into your mind's eye the person you are considering talking to. Then, in the visualization, play out what would happen if you spoke out. Let all the possible responses and recriminations unwind. As this happens, and when the scene is over, pay close attention to how shaken up you feel.

Then, after a break of at least a few hours, settle down and relax again. This time, imagine being with the person in question but staying silent. Allow yourself to picture you, and them, while you have the 'secret' in your mind. Concentrate also, on them 'not knowing' and how that makes you feel. Again, consider carefully what your emotional response is to all of this.

When you compare how each scene made you feel, there will be a jumble of emotions. But one will, hopefully, make you experience a wave of relief. This is your unconscious, intuitive mind speaking. It is telling you, bluntly, whether to spill the beans or shut up. If you follow its advice you won't avoid pain and turmoil, but you will be doing what you feel, deep down, is for the best. Knowing that should

give you the strength to cope with the consequences –
internally or externally – that will unavoidably follow.

Suggested Resource

Can Love Last? by S. A. Mitchell (W. W. Norton)

Dealing with Sibling Rivalry

Some claim being the oldest or youngest sibling in the family can dictate your personality type. Why are we convinced about the importance of birth order?

Are you an only child? The youngest? Or the first born? More to the point, does it matter? According to some theories, our place in our family's birth order is the crucial determinant of what kind of person we become. There are stacks of books offering different arguments to support this, and the idea is a popular one. But it is also mired in scientific controversy, and has been far from proven. The more interesting question might not be what our birth order position means for us, but why we seem so keen on the idea that it must mean something.

The leading proponent of the birth-order theory is Kevin Leman, author of *The Birth Order Book*. He claims it holds the key to our personality type, self-esteem, success and even intelligence. If you want to see whether the theory works for you, pick the description below which best fits your personality (the associated birth order is at the end of this chapter):

A. Mediator: avoids conflict, independent, extremely loyal to your peer group, many friends

B. Manipulator: charming, blames others, shows off, people person, good salesperson, precocious

C. Perfectionist: reliable, list-maker, well-organized, critical, serious, scholarly.

You've just done a scientific survey of one. Even if the theory worked for you, what did it prove? Frank Sulloway, author of *Born to Rebel*, claims to have studied thousands of people – and has also concluded that birth order matters a lot. He identifies an interesting statistical fact: most revolutionaries have been rebellious younger brothers. And he has concluded from his research that younger siblings are much more likely to do experimental, dangerous things.

The validity of birth-order theories has been called into doubt, however, by scientists carrying out 'meta-analyses' involving many thousands of subjects. After reviewing 35 years of research – some 1,500 studies – researchers at the University of Zurich concluded: 'On a scale of importance, the effects of birth order fall somewhere between negligible and nonexistent.'

This side of the debate is taken up by Dalton Conley in his book *The Pecking Order*. He argues that a lot of other factors affect the behaviour of first-borns and last-borns much more strongly than their place in the family. 'Early death of a parent, timing of economic shocks to the family, gender expectations and roles in the family, outside influences, random events, you name it,' Conley says. 'Birth order is basically at the bottom of that list.'

Confused? Welcome to the frustrating world of psychological research. The plethora of statistics used to back up one or the other side of any argument leads me to be very sceptical about the role science can play in deciding these kinds of debates. Sure, research evidence can illuminate. But I don't think it should be granted the role of final arbiter. I suspect that simple common sense – allied to our intuition – can often tell us more.

It's my experience as a therapist – a role where I have to focus deeply on why people turn out the way they do – which makes me a sceptic. I don't assume that the full complexity of someone's adult situation will slavishly follow their position when they were younger. So I am halfway between the two camps (and no, I wasn't a middle child). I think birth order can encourage certain characteristics – but that other factors can be just as important. Much more interesting, I think, is why so many people are wedded to the idea that birth order is the psychological Holy Grail.

I think there's a clue in the revealing analogy used by the sceptic Conley. He says,

> Birth order makes about as much sense as astrology, which is almost none. Just like in astrology, when you see a good fit, you say, 'Hah! He's such a Gemini.' Here you say, 'Hah, he's such a first-born, aggressive

*control freak,' but when it doesn't fit the mould, you
don't even notice it.*

I think we yearn for simple, deterministic answers to the
deepest questions in life. We don't want to think that our
personality is a result of a multitude of complex influences,
not least our own innate temperament or the way we
were looked after as children. We'd rather think that it was
all settled in the stars – or our place in the birth order –
because then we don't need to blame ourselves or our parents for how we turned out. If such simple matters determine how we've ended up, then we are not burdened with
any responsibility to try and change ourselves. Birth-order
theory is just a variation on the myth of pre-ordained fate,
and another excuse to avoid the truth that our 'destiny' lies
elsewhere – in our very own hands.

Answers:

    A = Middle child

    B = The youngest

    C = Only child or first born

Suggested Resources

The Birth Order Book by Kevin Leman (Fleming H. Revell)

Born to Rebel by Frank Sulloway (Abacus)

The Pecking Order by Dalton Conley (Pantheon)

Coping at Christmas

Do you look forward to the festive season with mixed emotions? Lower your expectations and surprise yourself with a really happy Christmas.

Christmas has a lot going for it: time off work, licence for over-indulgence and an unrelenting message of goodness and cheer. Despite all this, for many of us it is the most stressful time of the year. There are several interlinked reasons for this, and if we want to have a merry Christmas we need to pay attention to each one.

The first concerns our hyped-up expectations. Everything is supposed to be perfect and if it isn't we feel we've failed. If it is, we are often so exhausted from the effort that we can't enjoy what we've achieved. It will help if we give up on the idea that everything must be exactly right and instead accept that things just need to be 'good enough'.

On another level, we have allowed much of today's celebrations to fly in the face of what psychological wisdom tells us. We know, from countless studies, that material

possessions don't make us happy, yet the race to find the best and biggest present goes on. In contrast to money, things and status, it is good relationships that bring us real contentment and joy. Christmas should be a time to enjoy our family and friends, and this should be our focus – *being*, not buying.

But, of course, this is precisely where the problem often lies. Because rather than providing an opportunity for us to enjoy our closeness with others, Christmas often exposes how little closeness there is.

This can be masked throughout the year, as the hurly-burly of life and the modern extended family's geographical distance offer easy excuses for why we have become disconnected. But Christmas often throws us together, literally, and the underlying tensions spill out. Childhood dynamics resurface and these can cause confusion and resentment.

I know of one family where a successful woman visibly withdraws as the holiday goes on, until she is once again the dominated sister who has yet to eclipse her father and brothers. This used to be felt by her as a weird disorientation, but as the years have gone by she has realized what is going on – a powerful collective regression back to archaic family dynamics. She chooses to grin and bear it, seeking a quiet life, knowing that for the rest of the year the disappointed men in her family are only too well aware that she has outshone them. Her meekness, is, if you like, the best present she could give them.

In another family I have dealt with, the emotional coldness of the childhood home seems stifling to a particular daughter who has fought hard to bring warmth to her own family. She limits the time she spends with her more repressed parents and siblings, but ensures that, when she is there, she remains conscious of what is missing. She still invariably blows up over something inconsequential, but is increasingly aware of what is really triggering these outbursts. She still mourns the emotional closeness that she feels deprived of, but no longer lets it hit her anew every time she gathers around the hearth.

Both of these women are finding Christmas easier to handle because they are no longer kicking against what is around them. Instead of subconsciously expecting things to be different to how they have always been, they are consciously managing the depressing but potentially liberating idea that things will, almost always, never really change.

However it is manifest, and however you choose to deal with it, it is better to enter the festive season with your eyes wide open. So spend some time this year reviewing previous years' festivities – and the Christmases of your childhood – and see if you can identify the patterns that keep getting played out. When you have, then by all means be sad and angry that things have to be like this. But then take your lead from the age-old exhortation: 'Peace on earth and goodwill to all men.' It may not come easy but it's your best chance of enjoying some emotional peace of your own.

Suggested Resource

They Fuck You Up by Oliver James (Bloomsbury)

A Christmas for all Generations

Smooth over conflict and confusion for the elderly by reminiscing with them.

Our family is going through that halcyon era when Christmas brings out the best in everyone. Our three-year-old is discovering the magic of Santa Claus and the joy of exchanging presents, and her four grandparents are all relatively fit and well and able to run around after her while we eat and drink too much and watch the telly.

For lots of others, though, Christmas is a time of strain. Estranged relationships, sibling rivalry and financial pressure can dampen down any goodwill, but I know from sessions with several of my patients that, these days, there is another particular worry for many families.

Most of us have an elderly relative who is either in the throes of dementia or, while escaping that horror, has become curmudgeonly and demanding. It's funny, isn't it, how we are happy to deal with toddlers' tantrums, food games and attention-seeking but can't seem to find the patience to deal with similar behaviour from the other end of the age scale? How do we ensure that the *whole* family can relax and enjoy this special time?

A brilliant new book by psychologist Oliver James may provide the answer. He highlights a form of care known as 'Specal' (Specialised Early Care for Alzheimer's) developed by his mother-in-law. This rests on the insight that it is short-term memory that begins to dull with age. Long-term memory can remain largely intact. By allowing older people to live more in the past, their anxiety can be greatly reduced.

He gives the example of a woman who began to worry about her missing bags and kept mumbling about 'checking in' while at a doctor's surgery. She'd been told countless times where she was going but her mind could only make sense of the cramped waiting room by short-circuiting back to the airport lounges she'd often been in as a keen traveller. Rather than wrestle with this 'mistake' her carer simply reassured her that everything was OK and the flight was nearly ready to board. Minutes later she required the same reassurance again. She got it and relaxed. James calls this 'living in a kind of happy Groundhog Day'.

If your Christmas involves a relative with clear signs of Alzheimer's you should get hold of the book, but even if things thankfully aren't that serious, there are lessons in it for all of us struggling to bridge the generation gap. Too often this time of year is about the latest gadgets and fads, causing confusion to thirty-something parents, never mind pensioners. As well as enjoying all that, try and set aside time this year to dwell in the past a bit. Sit and talk of previous years – the great moments and the ones that went wrong. Encourage the oldest there to reminisce about their childhood Christmases – what were the presents like? What food did they eat? Was there snow to play in?

If you open up these stored memories you will find even the grumpiest grandpa or grandma slowly transported back to their past, and a look of joy and wonder will appear on their faces for what could be the first time in ages. Better still, there's a chance that any kid within earshot will be spellbound by such tales, and see their grandparent in a new light.

Suggested Resources

Contented Dementia: 24-hour Wraparound Care for Lifelong Well-being by Oliver James (Vermilion)

www.specal.co.uk

Lost Boys

Playing the field may be nothing new, but is today's generation of extreme pleasure-seekers really crying out for help?

When it comes to young men and sex, I thought I was pretty shockproof. Not just because I was hardly repressed in my own youth, but because of what I have learned since. During my psychotherapy training in California I worked with gang members whose attitudes to women were torn straight from the most misogynist hip-hop lyrics. For wannabe girl gangsters, being sexually available to gang leaders was a precondition of being allowed to join. I remember being staggered to discover that when these teenagers – some barely so – talked about 'hooking-up' they didn't mean dating or even snogging but having oral sex, or more accurately fellatio, as female pleasure rarely figured in their thinking. This most intimate of acts, echoing the disingenuous contortions of their one-time president, didn't apparently 'count' as sex.

Debate rages in the USA about the causes of this degeneracy, but we make a big mistake if we think the problem only exists on the other side of the Atlantic. In England, psychotherapy with adolescents is less common than it is in America, but I do often work with twenty-something men who feel they are struggling after their carefree time at university. Growing up, for many, seems hard to do. But I have also identified a worrying sexual trend among these 'lost boys'.

While some are in stable, committed relationships, others seem to prefer something quite different, and it's not just the usual 'playing of the field'. While it's a small, anecdotal sample, it's enough to worry me. Many of these young men exist in a world comprising casual sex with a string of girls they treat with almost no respect, near-obsessive masturbation to extreme hardcore internet pornography, and in a surprising number of cases, especially among those with money, regular liaisons with prostitutes. Now, maybe they will settle down after the sowing of these wild, wild oats, but what kind of husbands and fathers are they likely to make? And what lies behind their mindless pleasure-seeking?

Take Theo, a good-looking 22-year-old who happily confesses to sex with half a dozen Thai prostitutes on a recent backpacking holiday. He's slightly more ashamed of his nightly use of a website featuring older buxom ladies indulging in group sex with men his age and younger, but when he does confess this he can't quite hide his excitement. It turns out that Theo has never really gone out with girls, always priding himself on finding the 'easy lays' at school and college who, as he puts it, 'required no work'.

Theo's childhood was reasonably privileged, and unlike most of the young men I see, his parents hadn't divorced. When pressed, though, he describes a loveless marriage with eternal rows and a mum and dad chasing career success who rarely had time for him. He spent a lot of his youth daydreaming, smoking dope, masturbating and playing computer games.

Sadly, Theo's parents never showed him, by their implicit example or more explicit instruction, how to actually have relationships with people, let alone a partner. He lives with an all-encompassing mindset of self-absorption spiced up with regular low-effort sensation-seeking. There's no room for another person in this impoverished psychic world, just the occasional body.

Treating boys like Theo (for that is what they are, despite their gym-toned bodies, high-flying graduate jobs and sharp suits) is hard work. His big breakthrough came, no thanks to me, when he spent a few weeks with his mum when she was seriously ill. Unable to pursue her usual distracted existence, the two spent some real time together and that left Theo positively glowing.

This confirmed what I came to believe after working with those kids in America. All this frenetic sexual activity is actually a prolonged painful cry. What they want, and need, isn't yet another f**k but a cuddle – literal and metaphorical. Unfortunately, by the time a lovely if vulnerable young girl comes along who would give them that – one of Theo's 'easy lays' – they are too emotionally withdrawn to open their arms, and instead, yet again, just slide down their zip.

If we are not careful we will create a generation of men who don't just get their thrills from X-rated websites but live their soulless world out in reality — a world where mechanical sex replaces intimacy and love. And it's not just happening in the Californian 'hood; it's happening here.

Suggested Resource

Out of the Shadows: Understanding Sexual Addiction by Patrick Carnes (Hazelden)

PART 3

UNDERSTANDING YOUR WORLD

Motherhood

With research showing that the bond between mother and baby crucially affects the child's personality development, women face the dilemma of how soon they should go back to work. Let's look at care-giving in a time-pressured society.

As we prepared for the birth of our first child, we amassed a large pile of baby books. The thickest was the *Baby and Child Care Book* from Great Ormond Street. Its 600 pages cover everything you need to know. Yet there is no section on the vital question of how long mothers should stay with their babies before going back to work.

That is not surprising. It is an incendiary issue, covered in confusion and generating huge amounts of guilt. But that is not a reason to pretend it doesn't exist. It's certainly a common theme in the consulting room, either from mothers wondering how what they are doing is affecting their kids, or from adults who wonder if what their mother did when they were children might be contributing to their current problems.

So what do the latest scientific research and psychological theories tell us about mothers and their babies? And, more importantly, how should that be integrated with modern life, and all its competing pressures?

The theory is simple, and flows from the pioneering work of John Bowlby on 'attachment'. This argues that the ties formed between a child and its mother, from the child's first months and throughout its early years, crucially affect personality development, particularly traits relating to self-confidence. We learn to relate to others and, crucially, to regulate and soothe our own emotions, from the interactions we have as babies and toddlers.

Studies have long claimed that the longer a child spends with its mother, the better off it will be emotionally, as it matures. The latest research shows that the quality of the relationship between parent and child actually influences both the structure of the brain and the biochemistry within it. Repeated actions and responses by care-givers actually become etched into the baby's neural pathways, and provide the template for future relating. The scientist Joseph LeDoux is blunt: 'A few extra connections here, a little more or a little less neurotransmitter there, and animals begin to act differently.'

Let's get the guilt-inducing bit out of the way. It clearly is better for a baby, and indeed a child, to have a primary care-giver (almost always, in practice, the mother), who is present and available for as much time, and as long a time, as possible. Does that guarantee a well-behaved and emotionally healthy child? No. But the more the baby gets such attention, the more chance there is of that. If attention is limited, is the baby doomed to grow up miserable and unpopular? No. Many other factors come into play, and for the vast majority of mothers who feel they must – and want to – return to work at some point, there are several factors which should be borne in mind.

First, the necessary relating need not be done by the mother. That is what our culture traditionally expects, but actually, the 'continuous' care that Bowlby writes about can be provided by a father, too. Or a grandparent. Or, of course, a stable, attuned childminder. It can also be provided by a team of all of the above. That may not be as good as one primary caregiver, but what matters most is that the functions of childcaring – responsiveness, sensitivity, mirroring and play – are being provided. The more stable and ongoing each relationship, the better.

Secondly, there is the issue of the context of the maternal care. It is no good if the provision of maternal care is constant but of a conflicted or distracted sort. Sometimes resentment and boredom can grow, and while these are natural to an extent, and should be borne, if they become overwhelming then a mixture of work and childcare might actually be better than full-time childcare in the wrong atmosphere.

Lastly, the care – whether it is maternal or *in loco maternis* – must be of a good quality. Sometimes the right way of relating to babies and kids comes naturally. Often, because of our own childhood experiences, it doesn't. Getting help from groups, other mothers you admire and books is vital. A crucial component of high-quality care involves playing with the baby. In the Great Ormond Street book there's a whole section on this.

When playing, relating or simply providing, mindset is the key. Getting into a place where you are mentally and emotionally present with your baby is just as important as being physically present. In an ideal world all families would enjoy all three. In the real world, compromises are inevitable. But all the latest thinking says that every hour matters. So be there whenever you can, and when you are there, really *be* there.

Suggested Resource

Why Love Matters by Sue Gerhardt (Routledge)

Fatherhood

With absent fathers being blamed for so many of society's ills, it may be time to reassess the vital importance of the male role in child-rearing.

I remember, just before our daughter was born, several people asking me how I felt about becoming a father. As well as the usual nerves, I had a particular reason to be anxious. In the consulting room the costs of failed fathers are a near-constant presence. Often it is the mother whom we assume plays the all-important role in bringing up a child, but the more I practise therapy and delve into people's troubled pasts, the more I have come to believe that Dad's job is just as crucial.

This plays out in three areas, starting with the obvious and ending with the more obscure. The first is the issue of dads taking responsibility for sharing the work of child-rearing. More are doing so, though nowhere like equally in all but a tiny number of cases. The rest are missing out on what any involved father will tell you is the most amazing experience of his life. If that isn't enough of an incentive, there is a plethora of studies that shows that kids with involved fathers are less likely to be stressed, mentally ill or delinquent.

In addition to 'doing your share', there are two other roles specific to fathers that are just as important to get right. These involve modelling masculinity and representing the 'outside world'.

Where dads have failed to model what it's like to be a strong yet still sensitive father, the consequences are clear. It is not just weak men, unsure of how to find their power, who turn up for therapy; men who have masked that weakness with an outer shell of aggression do too. They play at being men, and end up a parody of what a strong man really is. Then, of course, there are the women who find it so hard to find the right sort of man because they were never given an example of what to look for in a partner, who often end up drawn to these caricatures of masculinity – the so-called 'bastards' – in an effort to find either echoes of the overbearing but yearned-for father of their childhood, or to crudely fill the hole left by the absence – physical or emotional – of a strong father.

Having made the case for fathers who are fully involved and can act with authority *and* empathy, I want to explore a more esoteric but vital role that fathers have: that of representing, and therefore teaching a child about, the outside world. The father's key job is to show the child that there is more to life than the close mother-baby unit, and that sometimes, someone else will disrupt that bond and exert their own needs. By experiencing this triangular relationship children slowly realize that they are not the centre of the world (as represented by Mum) and that the world doesn't collapse when Mum is fleetingly not there. On this foundation a sense of being able to recognize and cope with the needs of others, and an understanding of the complexities of multiple relationships, are built.

But, especially at first, the father must be intuitively sensitive to how frightening this can be for a child, who, for the first nine months of life, and for the larger part of the first few months out of the womb, needs – and should have – unfettered access to a 'primarily preoccupied' – to use Winnicott's phrase – mother.

A father must strike a balance – not opting out of the family at this crucial time, leaving Mum and the baby to 'get on with it', but also not too assertive about his needs, dragging the mother away from her focus on their baby. Without that balance, a child can develop an underlying fear of the outside world. Too much of the former and a child can grow up with an over-inflated sense of his own importance, and an underlying fear of the 'unknown' world outside his tight little enclave. Too much of the latter and the child will think he counts for little, and develop a fear of the world because it seems to be all-powerful and capricious.

I know that many people will find this all very un-PC. They will cry that others can take on these vital development tasks, and it is true that sometimes they have to. But as we look at a society where discipline and respect seem in freefall, I wonder if it is this dismissal and devaluation of the father's traditional role that may lie at the heart of our problems. On some level we are all looking for a strong, patient, kind, firm Dad to help us navigate this strange and frightening world. The more of them there are out there, the better it is for all of us.

Suggested Resource

Manhood by Steve Biddulph (Vermilion)

Pressured Childhood

Rather than pushing our kids, we need to learn the value of idle time.

Sometimes there is a connection between the very specific and personal things you hear in therapy and the trends out there in the wider society. I remember being struck, when treating a very alpha-male middle-aged guy, that his strict middle-class upbringing, common for men his age, would now be seen as unusual and, by many, abusive. We spent weeks dealing with the echoes of his father's, and mother's, voice, ordering him never to cry. Eventually, of course, he did, putting it better than I could when he mumbled, through sobs, 'That's been in me for 50 years.'

Sometimes, alas, the isolated damaging feature of someone's life hasn't become outdated, but frighteningly commonplace. This hit me at the start of a recent holiday in Greece. We were trying Mark Warner's kid-friendly resort for the first time with our two-year-old little girl. In the induction to the high-quality childcare on offer, one mother – of a four-year-old – raised her hand. 'Is there a syllabus?' she asked, 'or a certificate?' The T-shirted young nanny looked confused. 'We paint a goodbye picture,' she replied after a pause. Undaunted, the mother said, 'Well, it should be more formal or it's a waste of a week.' Never mind sandcastles, jumping in the pool, making new friends – without a curriculum the holiday was valueless to her.

All this reminded me of a patient I once had who had the archetypal pushy parents. Enrolling her for music, ballet and riding classes, employing tutors and treating her school reports with all the trepidation of a soldier's mother getting a telegram in the First World War.

Unsurprisingly, this bright, lovely girl grew up to believe that what mattered in life was success. Accordingly, she held down a high-flying job in the City but struggled to make friends, have relationships or find inner happiness or peace. The standard therapist's notion that she deserved to be valued just for who she was, rather than anything she might do, left her genuinely bemused.

Once upon a time, though – and she grew up in the sixties – such parental pressure was rare. I am not so sure that the demanding mother on our holiday is that unusual anymore. Parents, schools and our whole culture seem determined to push children from an ever earlier age. Standing up against that tide is really hard. It's the last thing we'd want for our daughter, but will that mean she starts behind at school, never able to catch up?

Thankfully, the evidence, and the practice of other countries in Europe suggest not, and that carefree, playful,

relaxed early years actually increase educational attainment later – presumably because learning slowly becomes a pleasure rather than a premature burden.

But why is this happening and what can we do about it?

I suspect that, as ever, something deeper is going on. Our demands on our children are masked in supposed concern for them but are actually about our own, rather more selfish interests. It is easier, I think, in our rushed and disconnected world, to draw up a timetable of activities, pay the fees and drop our kids off at endless classes and activities rather than wipe the board clean, adjust to their pace and priorities and give them that most valuable thing of all: time with their mum and dad. Not, incidentally, 'quality time' – quite the reverse: what one writer has wisely called 'rubbish time'. That aimless, just 'hanging-out' experience that is what makes a good childhood so wonderful.

With all the pressures on us as we struggle to attain that state ourselves, unsurprisingly we find it hard to achieve it with our children. So that's my remedy: put to one side the pressures of work and life (and, for the moment, your kids, too) for a few hours and just hang out with yourself. Go for a stroll, visit an art gallery, sing along to a favourite old album.

When we have mastered the art of doing nothing, we will rediscover its value and be able to pass it on to our kids. If we don't we will be raising a whole generation like my old patient, and storing up many, many more tears for future therapists to wipe away.

Suggested Resource

The Price of Privilege by Madeline Levine (HarperPaperbacks)

Masculinity

Nowadays, men are more likely to seek therapy than ever before as they struggle to work out what it really means to be a man.

Let's lay one myth to rest. Most people assume that it is overwhelmingly women who see therapists. Yet my own practice is an almost 50–50 male/female mix.

According to a British Association of Counselling and Psychotherapy (BACP) survey, the majority of men would be prepared to have therapy. Women rank only 'slightly more likely' than men to seek therapy.

Are the issues that men bring to therapy the same as those of women? Depression, anxiety and addictions seem to plague both sexes equally. So does a sense of being empty, lost or unfulfilled. But men are often struggling with another, overarching issue: what it means to be a man.

Many men seem to struggle to integrate their softer, more childlike side with their harder, more masculine side. Instead of finding a way to balance these two complementary aspects, they end up retreating into one or the other.

So they either become weak, indecisive and (sometimes literally) impotent, or they adopt a belligerent, macho posture that leads to upset and alienation.

In his classic novel *Bonfire of the Vanities*, Tom Wolfe coined the term 'Masters of the Universe' to describe men who are outwardly strong and successful. I was a junior version of such a phenomenon when I first worked in politics. But I left a trail of destruction behind me, in terms of let-down friends and broken relationships.

I think that the depression that often strikes high-achieving men – and that eventually struck me – that they mask with overwork, drinking or womanizing, is really the depression of the boy inside them, who has no less need for loving care and attention now than he had when he was a few months or years old.

It took several years of therapy before I realized that my work, and the power-playing that went with it, *and* the drink, drugs and promiscuity, were all really toys. Inside, unbeknownst to me, the little lost child part of me was in the driving seat. Far from being a Master of the Universe I was more like a tyrant of the playroom. It was only when I reconnected to the child part of me, and was able to offer him the love and stability he craved, that he began to calm down – and my life began to settle down.

Like me, many, many men – maybe most – seem to think that growing up means setting aside the more child-like part of themselves: that sensitivity must be sacrificed for strength.

The reasons men think this are diverse and often mysterious. Some never got the love and attention they needed, and abuse or neglect (which can happen in the most materially-endowed homes) ends up compelling them to develop a hard shell, impervious to the softer things in life, which they tell themselves are not for them. Others had a smothering mother who made caring seem too constraining, and so they took refuge in rebelliously macho behaviour to feel free. In most cases, the absence of a father who has been able to manage these issues successfully for himself meant that there was no role model to look up to and learn from.

However it came to pass, a man who splits off his more tender side may well achieve great things in the world, and even have some fun doing it, but he will eventually find that he is missing a key part of himself. For if you are not in touch with your softer, more sensitive side, you cannot connect with that part of others, no matter how hard you (or they) try. And that leads to loneliness, dissatisfaction and, eventually, despair.

That is why I think men are increasingly turning to therapy. They are no longer content with the 'shell' that hypermasculinity provides. They want to rediscover their more sensitive side and, crucially, find a way of integrating that with their strength.

But, despite their growing readiness, most men will not go to a therapist. They will struggle alone with trying to become a full rather than half a man or, if they are lucky, with the help of their nearest and dearest.

So the next time the man in your life exhibits all his worst male traits, try and see beyond his bluster. Take a deep breath and don't rise to the bait; try communicating instead to his hidden, more sensitive side. Remember: inside every macho man there is a little boy struggling to get out.

Suggested Resource

He: Understanding Masculine Psychology by Robert A. Johnson (HarperPerennial)

Religion

It may not be fashionable, but embracing religion in some form can lead to a happier life and a more stable state of mind.

Religion is no less fraught a subject in the consulting room than it is in the wider world. In fact, as it so often revolves around judgements regarding right and wrong, it's an area many therapists avoid like the plague. But is it a mistake to keep God out of therapy?

I am struck by how many people in longer-term therapy eventually turn their minds to spiritual matters. This need for connection to something more mystical and beyond ourselves seems always to coincide with real progress in treatment. It is that, and the experience of my own therapy, which make me think that, handled in the right way, religion and spirituality do belong in the consulting room.

There is some relevant research. Virginia Common-wealth University Medical College studied 1,902 twins and found that those who were committed to a spiritual dimension in their lives tended to have less depression and a lower

risk of addiction. They led healthier lifestyles and tended to smoke or drink less. Their marriages were more stable and they took comfort from the fact that their spiritual communities — of whatever type — formed a network that caught and supported people when they were struggling or ill.

Other reputable studies show that people who pray or meditate have lower blood pressure, stress levels and incidence of depression. Still more incredibly, various studies claim to prove that having someone pray for you, even if you are unaware of it, can lead to better recovery from heart disease and breast cancer.

That's not to say that therapists should proselytize. When I first went to therapy in 1998, my therapist was as directive as I think it's wise to be. She never pushed a particular religion or way of thinking but she did state bluntly that, in her opinion, emotional wellbeing required some form of spiritual awareness. She stressed that this needn't involve organized religion. It could revolve around private meditation, immersion in the splendours of nature or even the enjoyment of music or poetry. What mattered was heightened awareness and a sense of transcendence.

I suspect she is right, but I tend to be more circumspect. I wait for my patients to raise this subject and then see my role as helping them explore their developing thinking. I try and put aside my own beliefs, though I am open about these if asked.

After exploring Buddhism during my own journey, I have ended up expressing my spiritual side through a local

Anglican church. So when I examine this area I am best qualified to speak about Christianity, but I see the same dynamic at work in Islam, Hinduism and other religions.

You can either take from the Bible a lesson of tolerance and forgiveness or a message of inflexible judgement, original sin and guilt. I suspect we gravitate towards the version that most chimes with our existing psychic make-up. Thus, religious belief becomes a powerful reinforcer of what we actually already believe.

It can also, at its worst, act as a replacement for what we lack. It is obvious how appealing fundamentalism of any creed would be to a young person beset by doubt and desperately desiring an identity and somewhere to fit in.

As ever, though, with this issue, one soon strays onto dangerous ground. So I will venture just one last thought. When it comes to spirituality, as much as in any other area that is addressed by therapy, our watchwords should be openness, balance and a little room for doubt. Because, without those, it is all too easy for the damaged parts of us to make our God in *our* image, with all the awesome consequences for the rest of humanity that that implies.

Suggested Resource

Reading the Bible Again for the First Time: taking the Bible seriously but not literally by Marcus Borg (HarperSanFrancisco)

Celebrity

Examining our fascination with fame.

One of the big debates indulged in by therapists is how much 'self-disclosure' we should indulge in. In an effort to be the archetypal 'blank screen' that Freud recommended, some therapists go so far as to take off their wedding rings and eschew any personal touches in their consulting rooms. Others swing the other way, happily displaying family snap-shots and readily talking about their own experiences in an effort to engage and educate.

I am in the odd position of being married to some-one whose profession happens to make her well-known to many. Kate is a wonderful woman, but her job as a GMTV presenter means that sometimes our – and therefore my – private life is lived out in the public domain. At times we are complicit in this: for example, we used a deal with *OK!* magazine to pay for the party after our wedding. Much more often we have no control over what is printed – Kate's pregnancy was splashed on the front page of the *Sunday Mirror* before we even had a chance to tell most of our friends.

In the weeks after my wedding it was fascinating to observe how this had gone down with my patients. A few seemed genuinely oblivious, and noticed my wedding ring with what appeared to be genuine surprise. Others hesitantly enquired whether they might offer congratulations – desirous, I think, to bring into the room the fact that they had this 'extra-therapeutic' knowledge. I always welcome such genuine, commonplace human exchanges, though I swiftly bring the focus back where it should be – on my patient's life, not mine.

What needs to be guarded against is healthy, natural curiosity turning into unhealthy preoccupation. That would, I think, be reflecting something increasingly prevalent in modern society: an obsession with celebrities – A list and Z list – that seems to have taken on a pathological bent.

There is a voracious appetite for magazines devoted to paparazzi shots, tabloid gossip columns and 'kiss-and-tells'. At the 'A' end we elevate the likes of Brad Pitt to the status of gods. At the 'Z' end we are in danger of recreating the Victorian freak show in glorious Technicolor. We seem happiest when we can dump someone from one end of this scale to the other and back again, as happened recently with Kate Moss.

But what drives this fascination with other people who we know are, at least in part, media- and self-created concoctions? Why do we spend so much of our libido – our life energy – absorbed in following, discussing and getting worked up about celebrities?

I think that the clue to our obsession with scandal and gossip lies in an analysis of what goes on the mind of a celebrity stalker.

Celebrity stalkers lose their sense of boundaries – they begin to believe in the fantasy that they already know their star prey, or that the celebrity in question is just waiting to get to know them. On a deeper level I think the stalker, without realizing it, projects a part of themselves onto their victim. At that point the stalker ceases to see that they and their victim are separate. The stalker doesn't realize he or she is doing this, it is happening at a deep unconscious level.

The celebrity becomes the idealized, successful, loved person the stalker so much wants to be. At the same time, paradoxically, they project onto their victim the wounding, rejecting person who is actually a part of the stalker's own personality.

Why does this happen? Well, disturbing though it is to deal with these parts of yourself projected onto others, it is more tolerable, and controllable, than having them inside, where you have no distance from them at all.

And I don't think just stalkers do this. I think this dynamic lies at the heart of what the rest of us are doing, too. We invest in celebrities parts of ourselves, and their trials and tribulations become a substitute for living our own, full emotional lives.

This tendency is encouraged by the increasingly shallow and hollow nature of modern life. The lack of spirituality, the intoxication of consumerism and the breakdown of traditional family and community structures all contribute to rising numbers of people coming to therapy feeling lost, rootless and devoid of hope. People feel disconnected from others and the wider society in which they live.

So we look elsewhere for connection. A bit of fan worship is natural and healthy, but there is an undercurrent to our present obsession with celebrity. It is as if society as a whole has become a crazed stalker, so that we are seeking to live out our lives through 'them' rather than through ourselves.

In the consulting room, a good therapist tries to break down such vicarious fantasies and get the patient to reclaim the different parts of themselves and find the strength and ability to experience joy, love, jealousy, hatred – all the emotions – for themselves, in relation to the people they are intimate with in reality – not via relationships with media fantasy figures.

Indulging in a bit of celebrity-watching is harmless enough, and my wife and I both indulge and contribute at times. But when celebrity culture starts to crowd out everything else, maybe a re-focus is required – not just by celebrity stalkers but by society as a whole.

Suggested Resource

Illusions of Immortality: A Psychology of Fame and Celebrity by David Giles (Palgrave Macmillan)

What's So Fascinating about Britney?

Our voyeuristic interest in Britney Spears's public downfall reveals our own hidden envy.

Britney Spears appears special and – in the sense that we all get to participate as voyeurs in her suffering – she is. Her pain, though, is all too ordinary: someone is no doubt suffering similarly just a few streets away from wherever you are reading this. The brutal truth is that Britney's story doesn't – despite the millions of words and thousands of photos – tell us anything we didn't know about extreme emotional distress. It just puts it on gory display.

One commentator has said that because we know everything about a celebrity's life we now hunger for a 'new angle': that of their death. Tony Blair's old spin doctor Alastair Campbell wrote recently that some people are so famous they 'cease to be viewed as human beings'. There is, I am sure, some truth to both insights, but I am afraid I suspect that there is something even more disturbing going on.

What the tragedy of the once bright-eyed Mouseke-teer throws light on is that shady side of humanity that feeds on envy and destruction. For however much empathy and concern we might feel for Britney, our rapacious voyeurism is also that of the pack salivating over the kill. We can't look away because secretly we get a thrill from what we see.

These forces aren't just manifest through our fascination with car-crash celebrity gossip. One of the most vital, and difficult, tasks for any therapist is finding space for a patient's envy and aggression to emerge. I spent over a year with one woman who eventually broke down in shame, sobbing that she had celebrated her sister's miscarriage because she couldn't stand the idea that her sister would have children while she herself did not.

Envy is jealousy's more wicked cousin. When we're jeal-ous we just want what someone else has, and resent them for having it. When envy takes a grip over our minds we would gladly destroy the other person, and ourselves, to prevent them having something we cannot. It is the scorched earth of emotions, summed up well by that old song of the jilted lover, 'I'd rather be blue than happy with somebody new.'

While we often acknowledge our jealousy, our envy can be deeply hidden, even to ourselves. Time and time again I have discovered it at the root of disastrous relation-ships, whether involving couples, families or friends. All sorts of bizarre, hostile behaviour can have envy at its source. Lifetime enmities can be powered by this dark force, with neither party knowing its root cause.

Life Support

The good news is that once we have identified – and owned – our envy, it can begin to dissipate. Secrecy and disavowal seem to feed its destructive power, acceptance to weaken it.

So how is this related to Britney?

I think she symbolizes, when things are going well for her, a world of beauty, talent and wealth that stirs up deep envious feelings in most of us. She is, of course, a victim of her own troubled childhood and bad choices but, as I said earlier, that is her private tragedy. The way that the rest of us wolf down any public sign of her pain when she is at her worst allows us to give vent to the destructiveness that accompanies our envy of her when she is at her best.

We may think we wish her well, but do we? We may think we are mere witnesses to someone destroying herself. In fact, our very presence at the feast makes us complicit. For we devour Britney as surely as her own demons. And although one part of us knows it's very bad, to another it all tastes very good indeed.

Suggested Resources

Meeting the Shadow by Connie Zweig and Jeremiah Abrams (Jeremy P. Tarcher)

Why We Read 'Misery Memoirs'

Many of us are at least a little fascinated by other people's trauma, and the media is full of 'real-life' doom and gloom – but what does this say about us as people?

I imagine most of my colleagues, like me, see the recent boom in 'real-life' media misery akin to a busman's holiday. After a challenging few hours in the consulting room it's an odd therapist, I think, who would unwind reading a misery memoir like Dave Pelzer's *A Child Called It* or by watching *The Jeremy Kyle Show*.

But just about everyone else seems to have an insatiable appetite for larger-than-life horror stories – the more abusive and degrading, the better. Ever more traumatic biographies continue to top the best-seller lists; newsagents' shelves are crammed with 'true life story' magazines; and the TV schedules are full of sensationalist and revelatory documentaries.

What is it about other people's pain that many of us find so compelling? If you're someone who devours these grisly tales, this chapter may make uncomfortable reading. Because I suspect that behind the façade of light entertainment, there lies a deeper and more disturbing motivation for your interest. It's one which reveals as much about the dark truths inside your own mind as it does about the abusers who mesmerize you.

To begin, though, we should acknowledge the more benign reasons why people enjoy this kind of material. First and foremost, it affirms the resilience of the human spirit. People go through all sorts of trauma but live to tell the tale — and their stories reassure us that we, too, can survive our own more petty problems. There's also the sense of perspective we gain from it. Our own troubles can seem so much easier to cope with, compared to the terrors these poor unfortunate others have to suffer.

Exactly this same dynamic can be found at work in age-old myths, and in religions, too; just think of the labours of Hercules, or the biblical ordeal of Joseph. Indeed, the autobiographical nature of 'misery memoirs' may be new, but I suspect that most of Charles Dickens's novels probably fulfilled a similar function in an earlier age. Oliver Twist's tale of woe would sit happily in any modern-day 'real life' magazine spread. These stories all carry the same timelessly alluring message of redemption: people can live through adversity and ultimately thrive.

These are the sort of lofty claims the publishers of these books often make, quite reasonably, on their behalf. This material's appeal, however, also includes some rather

baser human motivations. Voyeurism definitely plays a part – and there's undoubtedly a touch of *schadenfreude* at work, too. On some level, we're celebrating our lucky escape from such dreadful experiences, secretly thinking to ourselves 'I'm glad that happened to them, and not me.' But our pleasure in these tales can often go far deeper, and to a much darker place, than that.

A key function of these traumatic horror stories, I believe, is that they allow us to indulge – vicariously, and almost completely unconsciously – an aspect of our humanity which is kept all but hidden in modern civilized society. They satisfy our impulse for aggression and cruelty. We would never dream of doing what these serial abusers do, of course – but, when we read about them, we stand for a moment in their shoes. Their acts revolt us, but they also – and you can see this in the faces of people reading these books, or in the frenzy of a Jerry Springer audience – excite us. Something about them stirs our most primeval selves.

For most of us, the beauty of being alive today is that we don't have to rely on our violent, animalistic instincts in order to survive. But because we still carry those feelings deep within us, we need an outlet for this subterranean part of our psyche. We've found it in these tales of torture and torment. They let us dwell for a while in the darkest vestige of our human heritage – but just when we might become frighteningly aware of what we're doing, we can switch channels or close the book. And return to 'civilization'.

Suggested Resource

Owning Your Own Shadow: Understanding the Dark Side of the Psyche
by Robert A. Johnson (HarperSanFrancisco)

Coping with Recession

When times are tough, can we find inner riches to help us get through?

Now might seem the worst possible time to suggest that we are too attached to material things. Many of us are at risk of losing our jobs, and all of us are experiencing a frightening fall in the value of our greatest asset, our house.

But psychotherapy is never at its strongest when it merely offers reassurance. Facing up to the worst, working through it and challenging conventional wisdom are the ingredients of good therapy, even if sometimes we resist all three.

Take one of my patients, who has been told that she won't be getting her usual five-figure annual bonus. In her mind she'd already spent this, on a new kitchen, and was disappointed and quite angry that she was going to be deprived.

Or another patient, a more serious situation, this one, who has lost his job in publishing and is afraid he might lose his home if he doesn't find a new position quickly. There's no doubt that, in this case, he is right to feel upset and afraid.

It would be unhelpful in the extreme to simply point out that he won't be left homeless; he'd get help with his mortgage payments, or if worse came to worst be able to find somewhere to live. Nor would it help to point out that such difficulties would pass: he's a highly able, skilled, relatively young man who would certainly pick up work once the recession is over.

Neither, though, would I serve him well simply by echoing his own sense of doom. Getting that balance right – of meeting a patient's pain while offering some relief and hope – is the art of being a good therapist, and sometimes we don't get it right.

What worked, after the initial sympathy, with both of these patients was a gentle opening up of the idea that they still had good things in their lives. It's a fine line to tread between the trite and the useful.

With my woman patient it was easier. She knew, deep down, that she didn't need a new kitchen, and some of her emotions masked fear that for her, too, things might get worse. When we looked at what she still had she alighted on a great idea. She would spend the very small bonus she had been given on a set of lovely picture frames, and put up photographs of her friends and family all over her old kitchen. In that way, in an emotional sense, she'd get a 'new' kitchen after all.

For the man I was treating, things had already got worse and there wasn't, alas, such an easy answer on offer. But after we talked things through he recognized that his happiness

didn't depend totally on his job and its financial rewards. He, his wife and their young toddler could – and would – survive a forced downsizing. He had some savings and a supportive family who would help out.

The message runs the risk of sounding trite, but I am afraid we still need to hear it. In times of recession we have to remember that there is more to life than money and possessions. We all can draw on the emotional and spiritual side of life rather than the purely material one.

Many of us face losing a lot in the current recession, and at times it will feel like we are losing everything. The sadness, anger and fear that comprise that 'losing everything' feeling must be acknowledged, but it is also necessary for us to recognize that it isn't really true. We will hurt, yes, but we will all survive.

Suggested Resource

Affluenza by Oliver James (Vermilion)

Reality TV

Psychology is now a fixture of the television schedules, and has brought therapy to a wider audience. But are TV producers taking risks with people's emotions?

Rarely a month goes by in which I am not offered a chance to be a TV shrink. The latest invitation was to travel to Australia with a group of delinquent teenagers. Before that I was asked to host a programme modelled on addiction-style 'interventions', where a person's nearest and dearest ambush them and force them into treatment.

I almost always decline, partly out of practicalities – who would look after my patients while I analysed teens in the outback? – but also because the kind of therapy I do isn't the sort that offers quick fixes. I got my need to live by soundbites out of my system when I first worked in politics.

But there's no doubt that in the last few years there has been an explosion in TV psychology. From Dr Tanya Byron on *Little Angels* to Benjamin Fry on *Spendaholics* to

the experts on *My Childhood*, the television schedules are crammed with programmes showcasing different kinds of therapy. Makeover shows for the soul are the latest version of reality TV, and often make for compelling viewing. But are these programmes always helpful?

Therapists' views are divided on this new phenomenon. Some worry about the dumbing down and exploitation that sometimes take place, whereas others are grateful that the potential of therapy, and a more psychologically-aware approach to life, are being brought to a wider audience. For myself, I have certainly noticed that patients will sometimes make reference to one of these programmes during sessions, and am certain that at least one current patient was inspired by them to seek actual therapy. So surely that must be a good thing?

But ethical questions do arise. I have serious doubts about the 'interventions' show, for example, because such an emotionally shocking and raw drama is probably best conducted in private. I am very glad, though, that many shows offer ongoing counselling to their participants, to help them deal with feelings stirred up long after the cameras have ceased to roll. In my view Ofcom should make such provision an obligation of all such shows.

But even where programmes provide proper support, the emotional impact should not be underestimated. TV hardman Jeremy Paxman was recently reduced to tears while filming the show *Who Do You Think You Are?* And I remember my then-boss Peter Mandelson crying when questioned about his father by the original (and still the best, in my view) TV psychologist Oliver James. It was something he would never talk about afterwards, not even to those closest to him, but millions had seen it happen.

Often these programmes unearth deep-seated emotional issues that the participants were unaware of when they originally agreed to take part. In *Little Angels*, for example, it is extraordinary how often Tanya Byron, once she has dispensed her wise parenting advice, discovers a deeper issue involving the trauma of one (or both) parents' childhoods which is reverberating through the generations. It is a phenomenon known in psychotherapy as 'ghosts in the nursery'. If a parent's own trauma isn't exorcised, it will almost inevitably be passed on.

The idea that our early development affects who we are today is the explicit assumption behind the BBC3 programme *My Childhood*, where the psychiatrist and celebrity act as psychological detectives, piecing together clues to their adult behaviour in the detritus of their childhoods. In this respect, the celebrities at least understand what they are getting themselves into – but they still risk being taken by emotional surprise on camera.

Some therapists are purists, and argue that all such work should be reserved for the consulting room. But not all the participants in these programmes would enter therapy in real life, and in some places it is hard to find the right sort of help. Sadly, few working-class families have access to a psychologist of the calibre of Dr Byron. And we shouldn't overlook the other, wider educational aspect – that many viewers participate in the therapy vicariously.

However snobby some therapists may be, with sensitivity and the right safeguards programmes like this reveal what we in the consulting room know only too well – that our childhoods are never really over, and that if they involved pain, however seemingly buried, it will only ever be just below the surface.

Whatever reservations we have about 'confessional' TV, at its best it sends out the message that such pain can be expressed – and can be healed. It is a message that may be well known to every therapist, but could come as a life-changing surprise to many viewers.

Suggested Resource

Little Angels: The Essential Guide to Transforming Your Family Life and Having More Time with Your Children by Tanya Byron and Sacha Baveystock (BBC Books)

PART 4

UNDERSTANDING THERAPY

Do I Need Therapy?

How do you know if you need help? Why so many of us are still reluctant to turn to therapy.

A friend of mine runs a boutique management consultancy and they have occasional lunches where outsiders are invited to come along and pose challenging questions. I was their guest recently and gave a provocative talk with the title 'Why you should all be in therapy'. Now, this was slightly tongue-in-cheek but it allowed me to talk about the benefits of opening yourself up to the kind of self-examination that therapy encourages.

A couple of people spoke to me quietly afterwards. One had experience of therapy and was grateful that I had helped remove the stigma he felt. He said he was now ready to admit to colleagues that he had taken the plunge. The second person to grab a few moments wanted to know whether I thought she 'needed' therapy. I had to explain that I couldn't judge that from a quick chat and that she should find a therapist and explore it. What was interesting is how ambivalent she was. She genuinely didn't seem to know.

I have a stock answer for such situations, if the person concerned is quite well-off. 'Why not try it?' I suggest, 'Do four sessions, it'll cost you a few hundred quid, and take up, including travelling, about a day of your life. That's all you've lost if it turns out you don't want to go further. The upside is it could be the beginning of a journey that'll change your life for ever.' On this occasion, my rather trite idea was brushed aside and, eventually, after we had moved outside and away from her workmates, my enquirer confessed what was on her mind. 'I don't think my problems are serious enough. The therapist will find them boring.'

This is not an uncommon thought. It manifests itself far less, though, in people underwhelming therapists with their tales, and much more in many others not getting the help they need. The idea that you deserve help – and that you might find it – is the theme of a novel *All in the Mind* by my old political friend Alastair Campbell, who used to work as Tony Blair's communications guru. The book had a good reception, but what many people failed to realize was that it is based on Alastair's real life. He has suffered terrible depressions, alcoholism and even a psychotic breakdown. He has direct experience of the therapies he outlines during the stories that make up his narrative.

While some of the cases he describes involve terrible trauma like rape or facial disfigurement, he shows how a low-key sense of hopelessness or loneliness can be just as devastating. Many people considering therapy, who hold themselves back because they don't think that what they

are suffering from is 'serious' enough, really mean that it's not dramatic enough.

I suggested that was the problem to the woman I was speaking to after that lunch. As I spoke the words she actually welled up with tears. 'That's just it. Nothing has happened to me. I just feel so empty, that it's all so pointless.'

I had gone as far as I could outside the consulting room, so I encouraged her to think about what we'd talked about and we said goodbye. I don't know if she ever found a therapist, or if she did, what happened. I am certain she needed to, yet something powerful stood in the way.

Her reluctance must have something to do with the ongoing stigma attached to mental illness. That's why I spoke at that lunch in the first place, and I know it was part of Alastair's motivation for writing his book. It still staggers me that society conspires to create a situation where we run to the GP or dentist at the first sign of physical pain, yet millions of us grit our teeth in the face of true mental torture that can go on for a lifetime. There's no great mystery, really. If you think you might need a doctor, you go and get checked out; if you think you need therapy, just do likewise.

Suggested Resource

All in the Mind by Alastair Campbell (Hutchinson)

The Therapy Relationship

After deciding you need therapy to feel better, how do you find the right person to help you get there?

One of my therapist friends calls it 'the January tales'. She's joking about the growing phenomenon of therapists being deluged with enquiries just after New Year. It's a time of year when more and more people are resolving to sort their lives out and recognizing that they might need help doing it.

Once they make the resolution they face the difficult task of finding the right therapist. There is a lot to say about this: the NHS should provide more; the profession should be clearer and more welcoming; the stigma about seeking help should be further reduced. But I want to deal with a more fundamental question: what relationship – for it is one – should you be looking for with your potential new therapist?

There are dozens of different therapy approaches and each boasts hundreds of books about the way that a therapist should relate to their clients. There are several professional bodies to which therapists belong. To confuse matters further, patients can present with a variety of personalities — and different problems — that call for a multiplicity of approaches. Yet I am going to venture that the issue can be resolved by asking one simple question.

Imagine a man whose mother would endlessly interfere in his life even though he was married with his own family. It wasn't just demands for time and attention; she would find subtle but devastating ways to insert herself into his mind: the classic tactic being a phantom illness that would arrive, like clockwork, on his wedding anniversary or his wife's birthday.

This man needed a therapist who would keep their distance a bit. Someone who was too empathic, too 'there', conjured up unconscious associations with this suffocating mother and he would find it unbearable. The therapist needed consciously to allow this patient space to develop where he could relax and begin to feel and think for himself.

Another patient had suffered a lonely childhood at the hands of a workaholic, often absent, father and a depressed, virtually alcoholic mother. This patient was often depressed herself, and lived a flat, emotionless existence which she tried to pep up with drink, drugs and roller-coaster relationships with largely unsuitable men.

She required a different approach from her therapist. For her, an emotional holding-back would have been disas-

trous, echoing her emotionally absent mother and father. She needed someone who was able to be deeply and visibly engaged with what she said, thought and felt. She needed a mirror in which to see herself, to put words to feelings and kick-start the emotional life that had been stunted when she was a child.

A good therapist will be able to adjust his or her style to cater for both these types of client. Indeed, I was therapist to both this man and this woman, and they each made good progress. That is because my goal when with a client is a simple one – and it illuminates the question of what you should be looking for in your therapist.

The key to a successful therapy relationship isn't necessarily liking the person, or feeling comfortable with them. You are not seeking a new friend. What should guide your choice of therapist is a simple question which, once asked, almost always answers itself easily: does this person understand me? Or, in other words, do I feel heard? Are they able to offer me the right fit that allows me to begin to speak my truth?

If it doesn't feel like that, *never* make the mistake of believing that there is something wrong with you. There isn't. It is the therapist's job to meet your mind, however much confusion and pain it is in. Not completely, or even immediately. But over the course of that first session you will know, in your bones, whether he or she 'gets' you. If they don't, then, sadly, you need to find someone else. If they do, you are well on the way to making your resolution a reality.

Suggested Resource

How Does Psychotherapy Work? edited by Jane Ryan (Karnac Books)

Truth in Therapy

How does a psychotherapist know if a patient is telling the truth? It's not essential to know; what's most revealing is how we create our own version of reality.

In the TV series I was involved in, *Kyle's Academy*, five people came together to stay in a house for two weeks. I took each of them on a therapeutic journey, all recorded in intimate detail by the cameras. It was a fascinating experience in many ways – not least because halfway through the two-week stay the participants' families arrived for a barbecue. I watched the ensuing interaction on a monitor inside. It was an unusual – and privileged – position for a psychotherapist to be in. I'd heard all five tell of their nearest and dearest; now I could see for myself.

People often ask how I know that people in the consulting room are 'telling the truth' about their lives. Self-evidently we only hear one side of the story, but if the therapy goes on for a while enough is revealed to allow you to draw some conclusions of your own. You can begin to probe a little.

How come the 'always unavailable' mum is offering to take the patient on a weekend away? Mustn't there be more to the 'rejecting brother' who we suddenly discover has asked our patient to be his best man, an offer the patient himself has spurned? A good therapist uses these apparent inconsistencies to do three things: test the patient's assumptions and the narrative they have long built up around them; challenge the patient to see and own more of their own role in what has developed over the years; and help the patient develop a deeper, more integrated sense of their important relationships.

I should stress that for the therapist the Holy Grail is not simply 'the truth' as it is commonly understood: the actual, verifiable reality of what has happened, historical and present-day fact if you like. We also pay close attention to 'emotional truth' — that is, what *seems* real to the patient. When this clashes with or contradicts the other sort of truth it can be terribly frustrating, especially for the patient's loved ones. If you feel that you sometimes have a dissonance between what feels emotionally true for you and what, on another level, you can see is actually happening, or if you are on the receiving end of such attitudes in someone else and can't understand what is happening, let me try and explain.

Our reality is made up of two things: external reality and internal reality. This latter is, in short, the particular set of coloured spectacles (rose or grey or otherwise) that we all wear as we observe and process what we see and experience. It can also be conceived of as the script we all

play *sotto voce* in our minds as we deal with life: 'Things will always turn out for the worse' or 'People will always take advantage of me' or 'Men are only after one thing.'

If we are relatively healthy these scripts are flexible, and open to alteration as experience proves us wrong. If we are not so emotionally healthy, these pre-existing assumptions determine our responses to everything. External reality isn't allowed to alter these internal prejudices – indeed, external reality is twisted to fit them. People end up self-sabotaging to ensure they are, once again, proved right. Their lack of enthusiasm once again leads to failure. To follow the above examples, their self-evident aura of victimhood leads them to be ripped off again; and their mistrust of all males puts off any man who seeks intimacy, leaving them the prey of those who don't.

These patterns, of course, are laid down in childhood. They are the messages that we heard from our mothers and fathers. Not only the specific words but the setting we play out our roles in: sunny and warm if we were lucky, cold, dark or stormy if we were not.

Back in *Kyle's Academy*, some of those who came to visit that Saturday were current friends and partners and so had suffered the consequences of what had already been laid down long ago. Others were parents or siblings, and one could see the echoes of what had made each participant who they were that day – some influencing for good, some bad, most, as is always the case, providing mixed messages.

Successful therapy will decouple these ancient scripts from present-day reality and allow room for reappraisal, change and growth. I decided to take part in the programme because I wanted to show a mass audience how therapy can work – and how we can better handle our emotional problems. I think I managed to do that, certainly in three out of five cases. But you don't have to take my word for it. Unlike normal therapy, which takes place behind closed doors, this time anyone who saw the programme can be the judge of what is 'true'.

Suggested Resource

What's Really Going on Here?: Making sense of our emotional lives by Susie Orbach (Virago)

Love and Therapy

We can't control when we fall in love, so don't put romance on hold while you're in therapy.

It is a question that has come up with almost every patient I have seen who was, or has become, single during their treatment. Given that they are trying to sort themselves out, should they avoid getting involved in a new relationship?

The usual cop-out therapist answer is that 'it depends on the case'. That, as always, is true. But only up to a point. I think there is a more fundamental and overarching answer, too. But individual circumstances do matter.

I saw a patient once who was a serial monogamist, only leaving one (always unsatisfactory) relationship when a new one had been lined up. This involved, while being technically faithful, getting involved in entangled flirtations with various men. I remember at one point we had a cast of possibilities including 'hatboy' from her office, the 'dishy brother' of one of her friends, and 'holiday hunk'. All kept in play in addition to her supposed actual boyfriend.

Much of this patient's psychic – and, indeed, physical – energy was taken up with this cast of characters and it became apparent that the associated dispersal of her attentions meant she never got really close to whichever one she was actually seeing. Spreading herself so thinly was, for her, actually a way of avoiding proper intimacy.

It is pretty obvious that for this patient a halting of such a merry-go-round may well have been wise while we sorted out what its underlying purpose was.

Another patient was her virtual polar opposite. She had not been romantically or sexually active for several years. Even her last 'relationship' had been asexual (and pretty uncaring) for years before it ended.

For her the danger was that therapy might become a substitute for making the effort required to find someone she could open up to. This was less to do with any feelings she had for me (though these may well have been there as a hidden fantasy) and more to do with the fact that the therapy situation gave her a safe, easy intimacy that meant she didn't have to search for something more.

In her case a constant exploration of why she was failing to make connections with men, and her inability to take action to try and find someone to have a relationship with, were important parts of her therapy.

So, yes, the particular circumstances of the patient determine, to an extent, whether they should be encouraged to avoid relationships or seek them out. But, as I suggested earlier, these are overridden by a more important factor: that of what Freud, in another context, called the 'reality principle'.

For when, how and whom we fall in love with is not something entirely in our control. Therapy should avoid promulgating the myth that we can completely control our destinies, romantic or otherwise. Meeting someone we like is part and parcel of life, and life not only should not, but of course cannot be placed on hold while we engage in therapy, however fundamental and important that work.

I know that there are rehab programmes, 12-step meetings and even some therapists who try and get patients to sign up to abstinence from relationships for 90 days or however long, and I understand the reasons why they do this. For some patients, at the extreme, they may even be worthwhile.

But for most people – even the compulsive flirt I mentioned earlier – it is more important to accept that we can't necessarily control what happens to us. Our job, in life and in therapy, is to be open to new possibilities and enter them with our eyes – and minds – as open as can be.

Trying to ban romance during therapy is not just impossible, but unwise. We may well make mistakes along the way, but that is how we learn – a vital process not helped by deluding ourselves that we can artificially withdraw from life until we are 'better'.

Suggested Resource

The Art of Loving by Erich Fromm (Thorsons)

Falling in Love with Your Therapist

It's possible to mistake the therapy relationship for the relationship you seek in the real world. If we analyse this we can move on.

'I fancy one of my patients.' Shocking, isn't it? But it happens. In supervision with a more experienced colleague or in a peer support group, such a revelation is common – and believe it or not, welcomed. Because, like all else in therapy, it is better for our thoughts and feelings to be acknowledged and dealt with rather than repressed.

That is true, also, of the contrary situation, where it becomes obvious that a patient has begun to fall in love with their therapist. This too, difficult though it is, needs to be addressed.

For the patient is, of course, not really in love with their therapist at all, and neither has the therapist fallen for the patient. What has happened is what psychoanalysts call 'erotic transference', where we are seeing in the other only one part of who they are and projecting the rest. A 'patient' can be brave and inspiring, a 'therapist' warm and caring.

But the 'real' person may be different. My patients don't get to see my selfishness and fussiness; those are reserved for those who really know me!

In California I treated a very beautiful Italian woman. I freely admit that if I'd met her at a party I'd have chatted her up. In therapy, though, we were largely treating the scared, unhappy young girl inside her, who undermined all her adult polish and success. That combination of innocence and sex appeal is alluring to most men, and I felt its pull.

She, in turn, seemed to find my combination of strength and caring attractive. She began to flirt and describe her sex life in a way that I began to suspect was designed to titillate me rather than help her. I was still in training and, after talking the case through with my supervisor, I decided this 'erotic vibe' had to be addressed. This is always tricky, as to make explicit the implicit can break the therapeutic bond. Sure enough, in this case, the patient couldn't explore what was going on and fled the treatment.

In another case a teenager I was treating began to dress more and more provocatively and started leaving me notes that were more suitable to a high-school locker than a consulting room. When I said that I thought she might be developing a crush on me, she too was embarrassed but we were able to talk it through. What we discovered was that she tended to relate to all men in a sexual way, as it gave her a sense of power. She continued in treatment for two years and, together, we helped her shed this tendency and learn to relate to men without flaunting her sexuality.

In neither case, as you can see, was I really being fancied for myself. Acting on such feelings would have been a gross abuse of trust, akin, in my view, to child abuse or incest. But here's where it gets a little more complicated. Because only seeing part of a person, and transferring our deepest wants and desires onto them, isn't a phenomenon confined to the consulting room. It also happens, to an extent, when we fall in love 'for real'.

On a deep level we are all yearning for a mother and father figure who will love and protect us as the ideal parent would have. But we also seek an adult companion and sexual partner. Ideally we want all these elements combined. So a little bit of 'transference' can add depth and power to a relationship. But for it to succeed beyond those first few months of being 'in love', we have to look beyond what we are projecting and fantasizing and see the real person underneath.

If what we see is compatible with those deeper yearnings, but the main attraction is our partner's actual self, we have the foundations of a great relationship. If the actuality clashes with what we've been transferring onto them, or the person underneath our projections has flaws and faults which would eventually become apparent, we should move on.

That can be hard to do, though. Just as in therapy, the key to getting it right is self-awareness and a bit of self-analysis. So if you are trying to work out whether your partner is right for you, ask yourself a simple question. Is it them I love, or really more my *idea* of them?

Suggested Resource

We: Understanding the Psychology of Romantic Love by Robert A. Johnson (HarperSanFrancisco)

Coping with Shame

We all do things we are ashamed of, but it doesn't make us bad people.

One of the myths of therapy is that psychotherapists should somehow put their real feelings to one side. That it's unacceptable to feel hate or anger towards our clients or be bored or repelled by them, or, at the opposite end of the continuum, as we just explored, be sexually attracted to them.

But, inevitably, every therapist will feel these things at one time or another. Of course, the difference is that unlike other people, therapists aren't supposed to *act* on their feelings. But far from putting them to one side we need to keep them in the centre of our minds when treating people.

That's a fine balancing act, though, as much communication is non-verbal. I remember making an extra effort to avoid looking bored with a client, who was, in truth, a little boring. With another, very attractive female client, I became a little paranoid about *where* to look, as I didn't want her to think I was looking *at* her. Not easy to avoid, of course, when sitting face-to-face for 50 minutes.

We therapists need to be particularly sensitive to our body language and facial expression when our clients are telling us something which shames them. Disgust, the natural human response to anything shameful, is a very strong emotion, one of the earliest a baby will show. Even dogs and other animals readily communicate this most primitive of feelings.

Yet if a client is already full of shame it can be very important not to let a flicker of disgust cross one's face. Once the secret is out you can analyse it together, but to show a strong negative reaction at the moment of revelation can shame a client into silence, or even, at the extreme, end a treatment.

One male client of mine finally started to talk about his sex life, which involved visits to prostitutes and some extremely kinky behaviour. Most people, would, to put it mildly, turn their noses up at the way he got his kicks. He, I am sure, deep down, suspected that I too was feeling a little revulsion, but I had to make sure I didn't show it. Afterwards, he thanked me for not looking repulsed.

Later in treatment he talked movingly about the way that his behaviour revolted him, and, free from the heat of that moment of disclosure I could admit that I too felt sick by what he did. By then, he could take this feedback.

Another client fared less well. She had a particularly bad eating disorder that made her do things to food that would, if I went into detail, surely put you off your next meal. As she told me about it I felt I'd masked my shock. But she suddenly blurted out that she could tell I was sickened and that she was hurt by this. It was hard to deny what I was feeling, and even though I don't know to this day whether I had given it away or she had imagined it, she was so affronted she never came back. I later read that disgust can flicker across the human face in a millisecond and we are adept at spotting that instant on another's face. Maybe I just didn't mask my response in time.

Dealing with all this is one of the paradoxes of therapy. You need to be in touch with your responses to clients but how much of these you pass on, and crucially when, are what make our profession an art rather than a science.

I think that almost everyone, apart from real sociopaths, knows that their secret shame, if it really is bad, is going to disgust other people. What they want is not collusion in it; after a while they want to be able to talk about its disgustingness. But at the instant of sharing it, often for the first time in their lives, they also want to see that the therapist is not disgusted by them, just by what they do. That is a distinction that can be made over time, but not in the flash of an eye, which is why not showing what you feel, in this situation, is a vital skill for a therapist to have.

Suggested Resource

Healing the Shame That Binds You by John Bradshaw (Health Communications)

Holidays

Everyone has to take a holiday – even therapists. But a patient's reaction to the absence can reveal much about their needs.

Nothing better illustrates the variety of people who enter a therapist's consulting room than their varying attitudes to what are known, in the psychology trade, as 'breaks'. Only the most disturbed patients act as if taking a break is unreasonable, or demand phone contact or create crises in an attempt to intrude upon what are, after all, necessary and natural absences. But most therapists will have experience of such an extreme response. Equally, only a small number of emotionally undeveloped or self-involved narcissistic patients will use the opportunity to show that they couldn't care less about the therapist not being there. The vast majority of patients do what you would expect: they calmly accept the news and jot down the dates in their diaries.

A good therapist, though, will look deeper into what might be going on, because a patient's reaction to their therapist's actions can be incredibly revealing about how

they handle things in their life *outside* the therapy room. Between the two extremes cited above there is a wealth of responses – from which we can, if we are smart, learn a lot. In particular there is space to feel some annoyance, disappointment, envy, even hostility, and to express these 'difficult' emotions. Can the therapist make it safe to do so?

I always found my therapist's breaks a relief. There's no doubt that's partly related to the fact that I've always found therapy hard work. If it's working it's uncomfortable and draining. But my analyst in Berkeley, where I did my therapy training, used to raise an eyebrow at my nonchalance. She posited that there was something else going on: that I was also trying to convince myself – and her – that I didn't need the therapy as much as I did. That I could take it or leave it. When she made this point I recognized it was true. It was a way of hanging on to some sense of independence, of telling myself that she didn't matter as much as she did.

What matters, of course, is not what my attitude was to her breaks, but whether this mirrored something more fundamental in my attitude to other people in my life. My therapist went on to suggest exactly that: my emotional disengagement from family and friends meant that I kept myself just a little bit isolated, not bound up in relationships that I felt made demands on me.

We were able, over the course of the next few weeks – and again when other breaks were looming – to examine this tendency. Not just by talking about it, but by analysing it as it happened between me and her. What did I not want to say to her? What was I keen to keep hidden from myself?

In my case it was my sense that I became vulnerable if I recognized my dependence on others. I didn't want to acknowledge my needs. I wasn't used to recognizing, accepting or expressing them. Eventually, using the crucible of her holidays, I was able to do all three. On one level I still rationally accepted her absences – after all, she deserved a break. On another I was able to see that I needed her, at that time, a great deal, and did feel a bit abandoned by her when she went away.

The attention we were able to bring to all this because of the intense nature of the consulting-room relationship meant that I ended up much more able to acknowledge my need for those closest to me. I don't doubt I am a better husband and father now because I can admit how much my wife and daughter mean to me, and how much I need them in my life.

How we react to such prosaic things as our therapist's holidays can open up huge questions about how we react to our wider world. If we allow ourselves to dig deeper rather than gloss over such matters, we can see what lies beneath our instinctive reactions and, if necessary, start to change them. That can bring about a beneficial change of scenery that lasts a lot, lot longer than any vacation.

Suggested Resource

Towards Emotional Literacy by Susie Orbach (Virago)

Therapy on TV

Therapy doesn't have to be the long, drawn-out process it is often thought to be. It is fair to expect some major insights to occur in the first few sessions, as happened on ITV1's *Kyle's Academy*.

Having voiced my concerns about therapy on TV, as I've mentioned I eventually did take part in such a show: ITV1's *Kyle's Academy*. For those of you who don't spend the afternoons watching daytime TV you can catch some clips on my website www.diy-therapy.com. Part of my motivation for agreeing to appear in such a programme was that I thought there was a real chance that viewers at home could learn something from what they saw.

On this occasion, I have to admit that I learned something very valuable, too. Recently I wrote a piece for my regular column in *Psychologies* magazine which struck a note of caution about how much – and how quickly – we can change. The hothouse of TV therapy has encouraged me to be more optimistic. I also realized something that could be of real benefit to anyone considering psychotherapy.

The case of Tracey stood out for me because she neither made wholesale improvements, like two of the other five volunteers, nor made poor progress, like the remaining two. Tracey entered the Academy feeling disconnected from her family, consumed with rage that erupted, too often, at her hapless husband, and often suffering from feelings of sadness and a lack of direction.

On the programme I gave her some simple anger-management tools (also available on my website) and we spent three sessions looking at her relationships with her dad and brother. As result of this work, Tracey's anger attacks have reduced dramatically and she is enjoying a real renaissance in relations with her dad. On the day of her last follow-on session with me, he had brought her up to London and they were going to spend the day together. She says this would never have happened before.

Now, during Tracey's two-week residential stay there was various help on offer, and no doubt there was something about being away from it all so intensively – and being on TV – that affected her outcome. But she credits those three sessions with me as having been crucial.

What Tracey's case tells us is not that miracles can happen in three sessions of therapy. They can't. But real change can. Crucially, Tracey learned that it was *possible* to transform her life, even if, this time, that happened to just a piece of it.

I admit that I felt more pressure, with limited time and watched by the cameras, to deliver such a result. In the

past, in my normal work off-screen I would have been less directive and let things develop more gradually. But that has begun to change. I have started to work on the assumption that if people come to therapy, and I want them to keep coming, I should be trying to ensure that there is a quick result, even if it is only to a small part of their problem.

I think it is a fair demand to make of any therapist. I'd recommend starting your treatment by saying something along the lines of: 'I'm not asking for a complete turnaround, but in three or so sessions I'd like to see a real improvement in at least one area.'

What Tracey did on *Kyle's Academy* was set off in a new direction. She still has some way to go, and still feels low and lost sometimes. But, whatever the future holds, thanks to that initial work we did, her anger is under control and she has a new closeness with her dad.

The great news is I'm helping her try and find a therapist locally who can carry on the work. Tracey has set out on her new path. Yours could be just around the corner. But if you do decide to try therapy, don't hesitate to ask for proof that you are on the right track. I think a good therapist will rise to the challenge.

(There's more about finding a therapist who's right for you in the 'Conclusion – Where to Go Next?' section on page 197.)

A Healthy Dislike

What happens when a therapist dislikes a patient?

Therapists, of course, are not meant to discuss their patients at dinner parties or down the pub. If we did, and you were in the audience, you would no doubt expect to hear us talk compassionately about our clients and their struggles. But would you also expect to hear us use words like 'boring', 'weird' or even 'hateful'? Well, if we broke our vows of confidentiality you would, because all therapists feel like that about some clients sometimes – and, far from being shameful, it is vital to helping those we might be talking about.

One of the grandfathers of psychotherapy, Donald Winnicott, wrote a paper in 1947 entitled 'Hate in the Countertransference' that is still required reading today. It emphasizes the importance of having an *authentic* response to your client, and sometimes letting that show. He cites the case of a delinquent boy who created continual mayhem, in the aftermath of which Winnicott would simply say to the boy, 'What you have done has made me hate you.'

Countertransference is a typically obscure therapy term that just means what the client stirs up in you. It is important

to be aware of this, as it is a sure-fire guide to what they are likely to stir up in everybody else in their life. When it is manifest in the room, the spotlight of therapy can shine upon it and insights – and therefore change – can occur.

Paying attention to your hostile feelings is also important in another, crucial way. Time and time again I have discovered that the feelings engendered in me are actually precisely what my client is feeling about the world. So if I find myself hating someone, I always wonder if I what I feel is just an echo of their underlying emotional state – that it is *they* who feel hate, terrible hate, towards the world. If I find someone very boring I will explore whether they, at a very deep level, are bored by themselves – and life itself.

A man I once treated became more and more irritating to me. I couldn't really explain why. He wasn't particularly annoying but I began to dread our sessions. Unsurprisingly, he complained of a similar dynamic in his life: he felt disliked, unpopular and spurned by other people. I was just feeling what everyone else felt. But I reflected deeply on what it was I was feeling. Underneath the hostility I realized that, despite my nature, training and experience with every other client I've ever seen, I just didn't care about this man. Was this a clue to how he felt? I ventured an interpretation, 'Although you say you want them to like you, maybe you don't really care about other people?' He broke down in tears. He admitted he secretly despised other people, saying he preferred to be on his own and that, often, other people, as he put it, 'made his skin crawl'.

At that point the focus of therapy shifted – from the apparent injustice of how he was treated by others to how he felt about others and why. Eventually, as we explored his childhood, we began to understand where this all came from, and his hatred of the world began to ease. Sure enough, my irritation with him then lessened and he found people in the rest of his life less hostile, too.

If I had buried my rejection of him, not allowing myself to feel it because it wasn't something a therapist 'should' feel, I would have missed the crux of his problem. I have written before that therapy is, in its essence, a form of love, but for it to be effective, sometimes it also has to be brave enough to be about hate.

Suggested Resource

Through Pediatrics to Psychoanalysis by D W Winnicott (Basic Books)

Therapist, Heal Thyself

Nobody's perfect. Experiencing what my patients are going through will, I hope, make me a better therapist.

I must have met dozens of therapists, and I do not know a single one who has not been in therapy themselves because, at one time, they have had to deal with an emotional or psychological problem. Some, of course, continue to struggle, and many, including me, are still in therapy themselves.

Does this mean that they are somehow suspect? That if they haven't sorted themselves out they shouldn't be trying to sort out anyone else? Should we simply beseech them: therapist, heal thyself? I think not.

Of course there are points at which a therapist should simply not practise – for example if they are suffering from a bout of severe mental illness, a really debilitating clinical depression or uncontrollable panic attacks. But what if the therapist is suffering from a mild depression, some stress or anxiety or is still working on a drink or drug problem? Again, the severity – and its impact on their performance in the consulting room – is the key, but there is a good reason why such problems shouldn't rule out practising *per se*. This reason has to do with what therapists expect from their clients.

We don't say that progress is dependent on 100 per cent of you feeling better. We are, rather, in the business of strengthening what is healthy and weakening what is not. Just as we would expect a therapist to be able to function if they have suffered a bereavement or physical illness (after a suitable break), we should be able to tolerate them working while not feeling 100 per cent emotionally.

We also have to admit that there will be occasions when we are struggling with our own issues while trying to help our patients. I remember treating a young man in California who was desperate to find a woman and settle down. My own love life was in dire straits, as I'd fallen for someone who was engaged to someone else and I was, frankly, making a bit of a fool of myself.

I certainly felt a bit of a fraud, talking with this patient about how to choose healthy, available women when I was literally doing the opposite. But did my human failings mean my insights were useless? I think not. They may even have been sharpened by the experience I was going through. The point is that therapists are working on themselves just as much as they are helping their patients. That may be an uncomfortable idea but the alternative is too idealistic: we are healers, not heroes.

We want to model a way of living that says that you

can still function productively if you are struggling, confused, making mistakes, or feeling low or worried. We can draw on the resilient, healthier parts of ourselves, both to cope as individuals and to help others. If a therapist's own problems are continually overshadowing the patient's in the therapist's mind, then that is untenable. But every therapist, just like every client, is entitled to the odd bad day.

What we can ask is that the therapist be aware of it and, if necessary, seek their own therapy to deal with it. I have just started my own therapy again, after a long break. At first it was because being in therapy is a requirement of a second MA I am doing at the Tavistock Clinic. But after a few weeks I realized there were still issues I wanted to work on. Hopefully this will make me a better husband and father – which would be a fantastic benefit for the investment of just 50 minutes a week. But I also hope it will make me a better therapist. Not because I will end up being perfect, but because I am continually willing to admit that I am not.

Suggested Resource

The Impossibility of Sex by Susie Orbach (Simon & Schuster)

Conclusion – Where to Go Next?

If you have enjoyed this book – and, more importantly, found it helpful – you may wonder what to do next. One obvious step is to consider seeing a therapist, if you haven't already, and there is help below on how to do that. Alternatively you may want to read more. I would suggest reading the books mentioned at the end of each chapter that you liked. I would also especially recommend the following three books, which are the ones that my patients have found most helpful over the years:

> *They F*** You Up: How to Survive Family Life* by Oliver James (Bloomsbury)
> *The Drama of the Gifted Child* by Alice Miller (Basic Books)
> *Self-esteem* by Matthew McKay and Patrick Fanning (Saint Martin's Press)

You could also visit www.diy-therapy.com, the website I run with my colleague Dr Cecilia Felice. Many of the resources there are free.

Whether you decide to try therapy or just read more, I hope you continue to find the help you need and that you go on to enjoy a happier and more successful life. One of the key insights of therapy is that we sometimes have to feel bad things like misery and fear, but that we also have the right to expect to feel good things like happiness and joy. If the ideas in this book have assisted you along the way, I am glad — and honoured to have been of help.

Finding a Therapist

If you feel that psychotherapy might benefit you there are several ways of finding the right therapist. Sadly, doing so is not as easy or straightforward as it should be. You could talk to your GP, although, despite the government expanding NHS therapy provision, it is still patchy. If you can afford to go private (therapy can cost between £25 and £100 a session) then there are five main organizations that can help you. If you want to know more, visit their websites. I am sorry it isn't easier to find the right therapist for you, but do keep trying. I am a member of the BACP, but I know good therapists in every one of these organizations:

British Association for Counselling and Psychotherapy (BACP): www.bacp.co.uk
British Psychoanalytic Council:
www.psychoanalytic-council.org
United Kingdom Council for Psychotherapy:

www.psychotherapy.org.uk

British Association for Behavioural and Cognitive Psycho-
therapies: www.babcp.com

British Psychological Society: www.bps.org.uk

I would particularly recommend contacting the Centre for
Attachment Based Psychoanalytic Psychotherapy (CAPP),
www.attachment.org.uk, whose approach is similar to mine
and reflects the ideas outlined in this book.

Good luck!

NOTES

NOTES

NOTES

NOTES

NOTES

NOTES

NOTES

We hope you enjoyed this Hay House book.
If you would like to receive a free catalogue featuring additional
Hay House books and products, or if you would like information
about the Hay Foundation, please contact:

Hay House UK Ltd
292B Kensal Rd • London W10 5BE
Tel: (44) 20 8962 1230; Fax: (44) 20 8962 1239
www.hayhouse.co.uk

***

Published and distributed in the United States of America by:
Hay House, Inc. • PO Box 5100 • Carlsbad, CA 92018-5100
Tel.: (1) 760 431 7695 or (1) 800 654 5126;
Fax: (1) 760 431 6948 or (1) 800 650 5115
www.hayhouse.com

Published and distributed in Australia by:
Hay House Australia Ltd • 18/36 Ralph St • Alexandria NSW 2015
Tel.: (61) 2 9669 4299; Fax: (61) 2 9669 4144
www.hayhouse.com.au

Published and distributed in the Republic of South Africa by:
Hay House SA (Pty) Ltd • PO Box 990 • Witkoppen 2068
Tel./Fax: (27) 11 467 8904 • www.hayhouse.co.za

Published and distributed in India by:
Hay House Publishers India • Muskaan Complex • Plot No.3
B-2 • Vasant Kunj • New Delhi – 110 070.
Tel.: (91) 11 41761620; Fax: (91) 11 41761630.
www.hayhouse.co.in

Distributed in Canada by:
Raincoast • 9050 Shaughnessy St • Vancouver, BC V6P 6E5
Tel.: (1) 604 323 7100; Fax: (1) 604 323 2600

***

Sign up via the Hay House UK website to receive the Hay House
online newsletter and stay informed about what's going on with
your favourite authors. You'll receive bimonthly announcements
about discounts and offers, special events, product highlights,
free excerpts, giveaways, and more!
www.hayhouse.co.uk